Join us as we delve into the intricacies of the life of Garry White, a man whose desire to become an adoptive parent was crushed by both his choice to remain single and his brush with mental illness in his younger days that branded him inadequate to be a parent. Many other qualities are needed for good parenting and that is what this book brings into the limelight. If you know Garry to any extent (and you will after reading this book), these issues would not even be considered when deciding if allowing him to adopt children is appropriate. He is the most caring, flexible, mannerly, loving, generous man I have ever met and I am privileged to have the honor of knowing him and being able to call him my friend. Having him as a father would probably be one of the greatest experiences any young person could have.

—*Rosanne Haas,* certified public school teacher, San Antonio, Texas

Dr. White's book walks one through the trials and tribulation of a single man's desire to start a family and provide for children with no homes. This book discusses the struggles of a lifetime of a compassionate, gentle person who tries to adopt a family and is turned away at every corner. If they only knew him like I do, this world would be a better place for a child.

—*Joseph Haas,* Computer Services Support, San Antonio, Texas

GARRY WHITE

MY QUEST
—— TO BE A ——
SINGLE DAD

Thirty-Plus Years Trying to Adopt

TATE PUBLISHING *& Enterprises*

My Quest to Be a Single Dad
Copyright © 2009 by Garry White. All rights reserved.

No part of this publication may be reproduced, stored in a retrieval system or transmitted in any way by any means, electronic, mechanical, photocopy, recording or otherwise without the prior permission of the author except as provided by USA copyright law.

The opinions expressed by the author are not necessarily those of Tate Publishing, LLC.

Published by Tate Publishing & Enterprises, LLC
127 E. Trade Center Terrace | Mustang, Oklahoma 73064 USA
1.888.361.9473 | www.tatepublishing.com

Tate Publishing is committed to excellence in the publishing industry. The company reflects the philosophy established by the founders, based on Psalm 68:11,
"The Lord gave the word and great was the company of those who published it."

Book design copyright © 2009 by Tate Publishing, LLC. All rights reserved.
Cover design by Kandi Evans
Interior design by Stefanie Rooney

Published in the United States of America

ISBN: 978-1-60799-987-4
1. Family & Relationships, Adoption & Fostering
2. Family & Relationships, Parenting, Single Parent
09.08.25

DEDICATION

To all homeless children and
child victims of predators

ACKNOWLEDGMENTS

The author wishes to acknowledge Kevin Kerrigan, Joseph Haas, and Rosanne Haas for their help in editing the chapters in this book.

For privacy reasons, identifiable information has been changed. Timeline was changed for continuity needs.

TABLE OF CONTENTS

Foreword 15

Prologue: Getting to Know Me 17

The Quest Begins 25
    Grandpa 25
    The Facts of Life 27
    The Wake-Up Call 29
    If a Monkey Can Do It, I Can Too 30
    The First Homeless Boy 31

The Single Foster Dad 39
    A Better Placement 44

The Grief of a Weekend Single Dad 47

Boy Scout Troop 848 55
    Wood Badge 58
    Scout Summer Camp 59
    Getting into Troop 848 61
    Campout Number One—Solve Problems 64
    Campout Number Two—Not be a Burden
        on Others 64
    Campout Number Three—What the
        Boy Scouts Learned 65
    Campout Number Four—How to Stop
        Two Boys' Fighting 66
    Campout Number Five—How to Deal with
        a Hyperactive Teenager 67
    Grand Canyon Goal Realized 67

Boy Scout Troop YCF: Bad Boys in Prison 71
YCF Experience Number One 75
YCF Experience Number Two 76
YCF Experience Number Three 77

Try Every Five Years for Twenty-Four Years 81
Try Again: 1989 81
Try Again: 1994 84
Try Again: 2001 84
Try Again: 2002—Private Agency
    Rimstone Adoptions—Domestic
    Again 89

Try Again Internationally 93
Early 2004: Rimstone International
    Adoption Agency 93
Late 2004: Agency Parent Maker
    and Immigration 97

Plan B: The Tucker Family   107
Grand Canyon 109
Weekend Substitute Parent 110
Harvey 110
Al 112
Wes 114
Christmas 116
A Problem or a Gift? 116
Supporting My Quest 117

My Big Final Try: International Again   121
References 124
Another Home Study 126
Immigration 128

Now What? The Big Debate 131
Decision for Second Application 131
Second Appeal 132
The Five Rimstone Concerns 133
Why Two or Three Children? 140
My Brother's Position 141
Fox's Appeal Brief 143

Plan B Again 147
My Rebuttal 149
Implementing Plan B Again 154
Another Big Hike 156
Ceremony of Loss 161

Section 504 and Me 163

Another Child Victim 171

Epilogue: The Best and True Dad 177
My Comparison to a
   Two-Parent Family 177
My Dreams Are Now a Fantasy 179
Continuing My Quest 181

Appendix A: My Letter to Rimstone Adoption Agency 183

Appendix B: Tips to Become a Single Adoptive Dad 185

Bibliography 193

FOREWORD

Welcome to the world of Garry White.

It's a weekday world of scholarly pursuits at a medium-sized central Texas university, full of teaching, writing, and counseling of students. On the weekends it's a world of tubing down a pristine river that flows directly through his backyard. There are also caves to explore and friends and family (he's a twin) to spend time with. He has worked with the Boy Scouts at a youth correctional faculty and was a single foster parent and a member of the Kiwanis Club. He has led several groups on hikes across the Grand Canyon and is a court-appointed special advocate (CASA) for children in foster care.

But it's also a world of anger, sadness, and frustration. Garry White has been trying for the past thirty years to be a single adoptive father. It is the one life goal he has set for himself that he has not attained. That's not to say he hasn't tried. He has battled governmental bureaucracy and mindless stereotyping almost from the minute he decided to become an adoptive parent.

You'll find out that it is not enough to have a good career and be a highly motivated man who has jumped through every hoop set out for him by both governmental and private agencies yet has been consistently turned down in his quest to adopt. At the age of fifty-nine, his chances for an adoption are rapidly dwindling, but as he will be quick to tell you: "I will have the satisfaction of never giving up, just like a true, loving dad."

In addition to baring his soul in the most painful of ways, Garry also provides valuable information for those who are in similar fights to become adoptive parents.

Get ready for a rough ride through the world of Garry White.

—*Kevin Kerrigan*, newspaper editor
and visiting journalism professor for
the University of Texas-Austin.

PROLOGUE: GETTING TO KNOW ME

My name is Garry L. White. I was born in California in the early 1950s. My dad was very involved with my twin brother and me. We took many family vacations, and Dad was our Cub Scout pack master. Once, when we were driving to the Grand Canyon, Dad told my brother and me to prepare to see something we would remember for the rest of our lives. When I saw the Grand Canyon, I promised myself that one day I would hike to the bottom. Upon college graduation, I did just that with a college fraternity brother.

My brother and I in the Cub Scouts

School was a problem. In the fourth grade, I was in a special class for slow learners. Two high school teachers told my parents that my brother and I would flunk out of college our first semester. We both are dyslexic. I have the most severe form of dyslexia. Audio-visual teaching methods didn't work. By the time I reached the ninth grade, I was reading at a third-grade level. When one of the nuns at my high school noticed that I was good in algebra but poor in history, she took action. Through her, kinesthetic and tactual methods were used. One of the methods was tracing letters in the sand. I learned to read and write.

My parents hired a special education tutor to teach my brother and me how to read and write in high school. I still have the canceled checks for that tutor. Dad once told us that he too had problems with reading and writing. He told us he would be happy as long as my brother and I did our best.

Today, I am a university professor with a PhD and two master's degrees. My brother has two master's degrees in engineering. My high school teachers were wrong. Thank God for that Catholic nun who saw what my brother and I were capable of. We just needed a different method of instruction.

From college on, I have had an active social life. Right after college, I hiked the Grand Canyon twice with college buddies. I will always remember, on my first trip, meeting a Boy Scout troop hiking out. When my college buddy and I turned around to see them hike out, we saw a big backpack with two little feet bobbing up the trail.

Second trip to the Grand Canyon; I'm in the middle

My brother once said I have more lifelong friends than anyone else he knew. All of my college apartment roommates moved out on me because they got married. After thirty years, all of those apartment roommates are still married to their first wives. We joke that they would rather live with their wives than move back in with me. They all have children, and some are grandparents.

My former roommates at our college fraternity twenty-fifth reunion

Wives of college fraternity brothers and former college roommates—no divorces yet; I'm the man left center

I am single, not by a conscious decision, but by how life has turned out for me. As I have seen my friends with their kids, I have sensed a void in my life. I wanted to be a dad just like my dad was. One of the joys of being a dad is getting to do fun and interesting things with your kids like snow skiing, swimming, hiking, kayaking, and riding bikes. Physical activity is a must for kids. This is something I learned from the Boy Scouts: get the kids tired. In the evening, they will be too worn out to get into mischief and will sleep well. As I always say, a sleeping child is a well-behaved child—unless the child is sleeping at school or church!

MY QUEST TO BE A SINGLE DAD

Snow skiing in California

Rapelling into a cave at age 57

Exploring a cave, age 57

Cooling off at Bright Angel Creek, Grand Canyon, AZ

Teaching Cub Scouts camp food

Best man at my brother's wedding; note the vest

You are invited to travel with me on my quest to be a single dad. But hold tight. It's going to be a very rough ride.

The Quest Begins

Grandpa

As a child, I remember my grandpa telling me about his dad, my great-granddad. When Grandpa talked about him, there was a look on his face that told me Grandpa thought greatly of him. Grandpa really missed him. Later, my mother told me why. When Grandpa was around eight years old, his mother had to put him in an orphanage. That was around 1905. My grandpa's mother then remarried. When her new husband heard she had a son in an orphanage, he went to the orphanage and told the staff, "No son of mine is going to live in an orphanage." Although the staff objected, he took Grandpa home. Imagine you are eight years old, living in an orphanage, and one day a stranger shows up and says you are his son, and you are going home this very moment. That family story has always stayed in my mind.

My brother and I with Dad and Grandpa

Grandpa also told me about how he worked in maintenance at an Oregon youth correctional facility. He said the kids liked him a lot. They all wanted to go with him when he had to pick up supplies in town. Grandpa always bought them ice cream for helping. Grandpa stressed that one reason the kids liked him so much was that he treated them as if they were his own. Little did I know that I would one day follow in my grandpa's footsteps.

I recall my dad telling me once how Grandpa had taken him to the youth correctional facility. There, looking through a peephole, Dad saw a fifteen-year-old boy who was a murderer. Dad told me that really shook him up.

When I was twelve, Grandpa visited my family in Pennsylvania. We visited a youth correctional facility there where one of Grandpa's former coworkers was superintendent. The facility looked like a large campus with no fence. Mom and Dad told my brother and me to stay in the car while Grandpa and Dad went in to get Grandpa's old friend. I recall seeing a boy riding a bike, and I wondered why he was in this facility. He looked and acted like any other kid.

The superintendent suggested we have a picnic near a lake on the facility. While we were eating, a truck came by. I saw teenagers in the back of the truck wearing gray uniforms and coming back from working on the grounds. They seemed to be enjoying themselves. I had to ask my dad what happened when these kids misbehaved. My dad told me to ask the superintendent. He told me they were placed in a small room with a bed, a table, and a small window. They would have to stay in that room until they decided to behave.

The Facts of Life

To earn my way through college, I was a hospital orderly for five summers, starting while in high school. My first summer there was when I learned the real facts of life. At age seventeen, I saw another teenager, age eighteen, die of bone cancer. When they brought him in on the floor, he was in really bad shape, constantly in pain. The head nurse told me to sit with him and visit. Because we were close in age, she thought it would make him feel better. So when I was not doing anything, I sat in his room.

About a week later, his mother pulled the emergency alarm in his room. All the nurses ran to his room, and I went with them. His mother was holding his hand. He was slowly gasping for air. The nurses were on the sides of the bed, and one nurse checked his blood pressure. I was at the foot of the bed, where I saw his face. His expression has been with me ever since. All I can say is that he knew he was dying. While his mother was holding his hand, he died. His face became pale and blank. The look of death is not the look of sleep. Luckily, I did not have to prepare his body for autopsy. The cause of death was clear, and arrangements had already been made with a funeral home.

That same summer on the floor, a sixteen-year-old boy was brought in. He was in bad shape, bedridden and unconscious. The doctors were not sure what was wrong with him. As an orderly, I took his vital signs, cleaned him up when he messed up the bed, and gave him bed baths for a few days. What was wrong, I do not know. After a few days, he regained consciousness. He eventually recovered and was discharged a-okay.

During my summers, I also worked in the emergency room. One day, the police called and said a twelve-year-old boy who had been shot was being brought in. The parents were contacted and told to meet the police at the emergency room. The mother arrived first. There, the police told the mother her son was dead. She broke down in tears, and her screams could be heard throughout the emergency room. The nurses asked if she would like a sedative. She said yes. As an orderly just starting college, I could only observe.

These three experiences at the hospital taught me a lot about life, death, and parents. When I went home after work, my parents could tell I was really depressed. I remember telling my dad about the sixteen-year-old. Dad was very understanding and expressed how compassionate I was. He indicated I was learning a lot about life. This world would be a better place if more teenagers worked in the hospitals and experienced the facts of life, death, and parents.

The Wake-Up Call

During my 1970 vacation from college, a fraternity brother invited me to go with him to Honduras. It would be my first trip outside the continental United States. I was shocked to see the poverty. My fraternity brother told me that Honduras was the poorest country in Central America.

The place I was staying was about four city blocks from the American Consulate. One morning I decided to walk to the American Consulate just to see where it was and to know how to get there if there were problems. As I walked down the dirt road, I was able to see the U.S. flag from the consulate compound behind a high brick wall. As I walked farther, I saw a pile of rags up against the consulate wall. Suddenly, the pile of rags moved. A boy stood up; he was maybe twelve or thirteen years old. He walked toward me with his right hand extended and palm open. His left hand was withered. What he said in Spanish, I do not know. I gave him all my Honduran coins. He returned to the consulate wall next to the dirt street and sat down again. That was an experience I will never forget. It occurred under the American flag. For the next few nights, I wondered what more I could have done to help that boy.

If a Monkey Can Do It, I Can Too

For years, I kept wondering what my goal in life should be in light of my Honduras and hospital experiences. Then, when I was working on a master's degree in psychology, I read an article in the September 1966 *American Scientist Journal* entitled "Learning to Love." Here is what the two researchers, Harlow and Harlow, found out. A group of distressed and anxiety-filled juvenile monkeys were place in a cage with adult male monkeys. The juvenile monkeys were experiencing rejection from their mothers. The mothers had given birth to other babies. What happened in that cage became my goal in life. The research article states,

> "Large adult males will actually physically adopt these displaced monkey juveniles and hold them in their arms or carry them about

on their backs, treating them for a considerable period of time in a maternal manner within the physiological limitations inherited in the primate male."
Harlow & Harlow, 1966, p. 247–248

The caption to a picture in the article read, *Male bonnet macaque holding young juvenile he has adopted* (Harlow & Harlow, 1966, p. 247, Fig. 2).

If an adult male monkey could adopt a distressed and anxiety-filled juvenile monkey that has experienced rejection from his mother, I knew I could adopt a distressed and anxious little boy who had experienced rejection from his mother. My goal in life was to be a dad to a homeless boy.

The First Homeless Boy

Around 1975, while in graduate school, I was visiting a college buddy in his apartment. There was a thirteen-year-old boy there. My college buddy had become a weekend volunteer for a foster child under the care of Child Protective Services. His role was to take this boy, Matt, for weekend outings. Matt had just arrived at a group foster home. He was friendly and very sociable. A few months later, my college buddy was leaving to do other things and suggested I replace him as the weekend volunteer for this teenage boy. That started a relationship with a homeless boy that lasted for almost nine years.

For the first few years, I took him out on weekends and eventually, short trips. Over time, he warmed up to me and told me about his past. He was a street kid and had spent time at a treatment facility before being adopted. He said the staff coached the kids as to what to say and do when volunteers came and worked with them. One treatment, he told me, was lying in the lap of an adult, and the adult would hold him in her arms like a baby. I recall learning somewhere that this treatment is used on children whose parents failed to hold them as babies and toddlers. It can also be used, I believe, as a treatment for children who are becoming sociopaths or who have attachment disorders.

When Matt was around the age of twelve, he was adopted by a highly religious family, very rigid in their faith. Once he got into a fight with his adoptive father and refused to go to church. His placement was terminated when he had sex with the family's teenage daughter. He told me the girl was willing. His caseworker came to the house and told Matt to pack his things. Matt was taken to the group foster home where he stayed until he was eighteen.

When he turned sixteen, I started to let him drive my car in the parking lot. That was a mistake. One night, while I was asleep, he took my car keys and went driving. The next morning there was a dent on my car. He finally admitted what he did, and I told him I would never let him drive my car again.

One evening at my apartment, after I'd been working with him for about three years, Matt opened up about his horrible past. At the age of eleven, he had been on the streets. There he was captured by a child predator. Matt told me he became a "child sex slave" for almost a year. This was the first time I heard the terms *child predator* and *child sex slave*. A social worker rescued him, and he was taken to a treatment facility. His physical needs were met, but psychologically he was a mess.

Matt told me in detail the life of a child sex slave, the sexual abuse, and the torture that left no bodily/physical evidence. He explained in detail how the predator would tie him up and torture him. He also explained *grooming*, the process by which the child's appearance was changed. It started with a new hairstyle and graduated to facial piercing of the most painful sort. Matt told me that when the predator put a ring on his lower lip, it had been very painful. A jewelry piercing had also been put on his earlobe. Imagine being eleven years old, held down by a big man, having your facial appearance changed, being in agonizing pain, and no one hears your screams or rescues you. Matt called the hairstyle changes and facial piercings his *leash*, the method by which the predator controlled him. Who would believe a kid with facial piercings? As Matt put it, people tended to avoid him.

Matt also told me that when the predator got tired of him and wanted another child, the predator planned to kill him. Matt knew he was going to be murdered yet could not escape. I asked him why he had not run away. Matt blew up. "You don't understand what a predator does to a child. I was scared!" Worse still, he said, his predator lent him out to other predators for their sexual desires. There was no place to run, and again, who would believe an antisocial, rebellious-looking street kid, anyway?

Matt told me that "predators breed predators," that child victims often become predators. He was right. Years later, I learned that 25 percent of child victims grow up to be predators themselves.

The predator took him on outings. Matt said it really hurt to see other kids with loving families while in public. Matt met another child sex slave, a girl, when his predator was visiting another predator. She had a ring through her nose along with an earlobe piercing. It sounded as if the predators had a brutal, twisted social network.

Hearing the words *child sex slave* for the first time was a real shock for me. Years later, when I became an assistant scoutmaster at a youth correctional facility, the director there told me that some of the boys I would work with would be former sex slaves who had been tortured.

Matt was starting to have problems at the group foster home. However, the group foster home mother told me that Matt was a different child at school. While visiting the high school, she had seen Matt, who was in special education himself, helping the handicapped kids.

When he turned eighteen, the group foster home offered him a small apartment where he could live and be a part-time staff member. However, his behavior was getting worse, and I suspected that he was becoming a drug dealer. Something happened that forced the home director to call Matt's caseworker and tell him to remove Matt from the home. The group foster home mother would not tell me what it was. All I know is that Matt asked me to pick him up at the home the day he was to leave and drive him somewhere. When I arrived, the foster home mother and his caseworker were there. The home mother told Matt that he was his own worst enemy and that he had to change. His caseworker told me Child Protective Services was closing Matt's case file since he was now eighteen.

Matt got into my car with a small backpack. I drove him where he wanted to go. He got out of the car and started walking. He did not want me to know where he was going to stay. Some time later, he called me and told me he had a place to stay, with a physically handicapped roommate, and was in a government work program to pay the bills. I suspected he was into drugs. After about a year, the government work program ran out, and he asked if he could live with me. Sadly, I had to turn him down because I was a foster parent to an eight-year-old boy. I managed to get him into the Job Corps. That lasted only six months. He was expelled and was living in a very cheap apartment.

A friend, Mary, and I tried to get him into a rehab center, but he insisted that he had to pay his utility bill first. We took him to the payment center and sat in the car to wait for him. Every so often, he would turn to look at us, and we finally saw him complete a drug transaction with one of the women in the line. When he got back into the car, I told him I had to search him. He had marijuana and pills. We should have turned him into the police but did not. We just took him back to his apartment.

In the early spring of 1983, when he was twenty, he again wanted to live with me, but with his drug and alcohol problems and my efforts to adopt, I had to say no. He stayed with me for a few days. Again, Mary and I took him to a rehab center for alcoholics. There a nurse talked to Matt, with Mary and me standing by his side. It was obvious to the nurse that Matt was there only because Mary and I had brought him there. The nurse gave Matt the phone number of an organization that would help him and said that there were people there who would come and get him and take him to a safe place where he could get help and a new start on life. All he had to do was to call that number and ask for help.

When we left the rehab center, Matt said he was tired and wanted to stop for the day and go back to my place. He told me he would make the call the next day. The next day, Matt said nothing about the phone number the nurse had given him and waited to see what I was going to do for that day. Matt and I returned to the same center. While someone counseled Matt, the nurse took me outside to talk. He asked why Matt had not called the number he'd given him the day before. I stopped and thought for a moment. The nurse then told me that Matt was taking advantage of my good nature. He said Matt had no interest in helping himself, and he expected me to take care of him. That was really hard to take in, but it was true.

Then came the real shocker. The nurse told me I had to end my mentorship with Matt and walk out of his life. He said I had to walk back into the rehab center and tell Matt, "You are no longer going to use me; I am out of your life. Goodbye." I did so and walked out of the building to my car. Matt followed me, weeping, and repeating, "Why?"

I answered that he had not made any effort to get help by calling the phone number. He replied that he was scared. I told Matt what I was going to do with his belongings in the trunk of my car and how he could retrieve them. I got into my car and drove off, leaving Matt with the nurse. From my rearview mirror, I saw the nurse trying to get Matt back into the rehab center. I think he ran away.

When I got home, I sat on my bed and cried. Nine years of trying to help had failed. Matt did contact me a few times over the next year, but after that, I no longer had any contact with him. About ten years later, a close friend saw Matt at a school function. He was pushing a handicapped person around in a wheelchair. It appeared Matt had a job as a caregiver for the handicapped.

In 2006, I did a computer search on him. I learned that he was living in a mobile home park on the west side of Boise, Idaho. He had no criminal record except for one third-degree felony, which I already knew about.

In 2007, I told my therapist this story. The therapist said I had helped him by walking out of his life. The shock of my departure had probably made him realize he needed to help himself. As of this writing, I have had no contact with him for these past twenty-four years. But I know Matt is doing well. He is a natural as a caregiver for the handicapped.

The Single Foster Dad

In 1978, I decided it was time to try adoption. I had recently graduated from college with a master's degree in psychology and was a high school teacher. It seemed to me that my background and circumstances were perfect to be a single dad, but when I went to the state's department of Child Protective Services, they said I was too young.

The next year, I found a private agency that was willing to work with me. The home study went well, and I was approved. Within a year, they found a ten-year-old boy who was living in a children's home. All the information about him fit me. A visit was arranged, and the caseworker and I drove to the children's home to meet with the director and staff. There they provided more information about this boy. The caseworker warned me not to say anything to the boy about why I was there or who I was.

We drove to his school, where we met his principal and teacher. As my caseworker turned to talk to someone, I looked down and noticed the boy standing right next to me. I froze. Here was the child who might soon be my son. He wanted to know why his caseworker was visiting his school and if she had found a family for him. His voice and demeanor told me he yearned for a family. As my excitement built, we returned to the children's home and had a short visit with him on the playground. My caseworker said the visit was over and told me to contact her in two weeks. When I did, she told me the placement would not work and that my file was being closed. That was a shock.

Looking back, years later, I realized that my mannerisms at that time seemed anxious while I had talked with the home director and schoolteachers. The frustration of helping Matt was starting to take its toll in the form of anxiety over an adoption. Unfortunately, I did not realize that at the time.

A year after that failed visit, I decided I might not be ready for adoption and that fostering may better prepare me. In the spring of 1981, I completed foster training. My caseworker said that I seemed to be able to sympathize with the feelings of a foster child. She noted that I had learned a lot from volunteer work at a group home. After all, I had adjusted to a manipulative and disturbed teenager, Matt. I had become a consistent and reliable friend to Matt rather than a victim of his con artistry.

That summer an eight-year-old boy, Mark, was placed with me. He lived with me for almost a year and a half.

I remember the first day he visited me. When he saw me at the door of my apartment, he ran up to meet me, and I showed him his room. While he explored the room, the caseworker briefed me about his placement. He had been in a children's shelter for a month. He was being removed from his mother due to neglect. Paperwork had already been done, so he could move in with me within the week.

When he moved in, he had only the clothes he was wearing, nothing else. As he amused himself with the toys and children's books I had, the caseworker arranged to bring his clothes to my home. She insisted I take the clothes directly to the laundry room and wash them. I soon learned why. As I started putting the clothes in the washer, cockroaches kept popping up. I dumped the clothes on the sidewalk, and hundreds of roaches swarmed out. I wondered what kind of home Mark had come from.

Aside from the roaches, the first week went well, except for one evening at the dinner table when Mark spilled a glass of milk all over the table and floor. He looked at me with fear in his eyes. Finally, I said, "Well, are you going to clean up the mess and pour yourself another glass of milk? Come with me, and I'll get you some paper towels to clear things up." He eagerly got the paper towels and cleaned up the mess. I had to remind him to pour another glass of milk.

Mark learning to ride a bike

Mark and I on a fishing trip

As time went by, we enjoyed many outings including swimming, fishing, bike riding, and short trips, one of them to Mexico. When I helped him with his homework from school, I learned that Mark tended to get angry with himself when he made mistakes. I got the school to provide services for special needs children.

A trip to the doctor revealed that Mark's height and weight were closer to a five-year-old than an eight-year-old. The doctor and caseworker pointed out that a poor environment usually slows the growth rate. When such a child is placed in an enriched environment, they quietly catch up in physical growth. A year later, he grew within the normal range for his age.

When Mark got home from school one day, he had a flyer about joining the Cub Scouts. Great! Here was an opportunity to have quality time and involvement with my foster son. My own dad had been a pack master. Being a Cub Scout helped Mark, and I also learned something about human nature in the process. Most of the parents who signed up to help me as den leader didn't. I was left to create the activities for the weekly meetings by myself.

After four months, Mark started to show difficulty in accepting limits. He started to act out and have temper tantrums. Several times when he was having a temper tantrum, I placed him on his bed to let him kick the mattress and pillow while I stood back and made sure he did not hurt himself. Yes, I did spank him a few times, within the guidelines of Child Protective Services.

After six months, he started to have night terrors and kept crawling into bed with me. After the third night, I called his caseworker and told her. She asked me how I had handled it. I answered that my procedure was to put him back in his own bed as soon as he fell asleep. If I forced him back to his bed, his reaction to the night terrors would get worse. It got to the point where I allowed him to sleep on a cot next to my bed.

A Better Placement

Mark started to see a psychiatrist and was prescribed a mind-altering medication that helped improve his behavior and reduce his destructive fantasies. It was becoming clear that Mark needed a foster home that could better address his needs. My mother offered to take care of Mark while I took a trip to think about it. I traveled to Flagstaff, Arizona, and climbed to the top of Mt. San Francisco. There on top of the mountain, where I could see for miles, I thought about his best interests.

A coworker had told me Mark needed the love of a mother. So I decided he had to move to a better foster home. I climbed down the mountain and drove to Sunset Crater to get a picture of Mt. San Francisco. That picture of the mountain where I decided to give Mark up has hung in my bedroom for the past twenty-five years.

When I returned home, I asked CPS to find a better placement for him, a home with two parents.

As the caseworker noted, his needs exceeded what I could offer. A CPS report said I had done my best to address Mark's needs. CPS asked if Mark could stay with me until they found a better placement. My answer was yes. I was in no hurry for him to leave. He left four months later.

For a year after he left me, I kept in touch with him and visited him in his two subsequent foster homes. By mutual agreement, CPS closed my file in the spring of 1983. My plans were to pursue an adoption through a private agency.

Mark's new foster home was a two-parent family with children. Once, when the foster mother dropped Mark off to spend the weekend with me, she seemed angry and eager to get him out of the house. When they came to pick him up, Mark ran and hid in a closet. That placement lasted six months. I suspect he was too aggressive with their toddler son.

Next he was placed with a two-parent family with no other children. This third foster home was a few blocks from where I worked, and Mark's school was across the street. That lasted a year. When he was placed in a residential treatment center in 1984, CPS sent me a letter stating he was becoming confused and that I had to stop visiting him. I have had no contact with him since.

In 2007, I searched for him. Public records showed criminal activity. He spent thirty days in jail for a misdemeanor crime when he was in his mid-twenties. At the time, he was unemployed, with only a high school education, and living with a friend. He had no income or any financial support.

I cried. Maybe the decision I had made at the top of Mt. San Francisco outside Flagstaff, Arizona, had been a mistake.

I sent him a letter to the addresses I found, asking if he would like to meet with me. There was no reply. If he did get the letter, I respect his privacy.

The Grief of a Weekend Single Dad

After my foster home file was closed in the spring of 1983, I approached a private agency about adoption. I had just bought a house, and after my experience with fostering, I was ready to bring home a homeless boy as my son. At first, I was skeptical about whether the agency would accept me since Mark's problems had exceeded what I could do for him. But the agency rated me "acceptable," and in the early fall of 1983, my caseworker called and said she had papers for me to review on a twelve-year-old boy living in a children's home three hundred miles away. We will call him Luke.

I told my caseworker that I wanted to look at his picture after I reviewed his paperwork. This was to ensure objectivity. His paperwork was acceptable. The only noted characteristic was that he did not talk much. When I looked at his picture, I knew I had found my son. Arrangements were made for me to visit him at the children's home several hundred miles away.

When I arrived at the home, the director took Luke's caseworker and me to his office. Then the boy came in and sat on the couch across from me. He was smiling but did not say anything. The director asked if he would like to go to the mall for an outing with me. He said yes and appeared pleased.

At the mall, we came to a toy store, and I told him to go in to look at the toys. I would stay near the front door. I got him to walk down one of the aisles and went back to the front door. When I turned around, he was standing right behind me. Again, I got him to go down an aisle. When I turned around again, he was there just standing next to me. I asked why he did not want to look at the toys.

He said, "I want to stay close to you."

My heart just fell. Here was a boy who felt safe with me. I smiled, and we both went down the aisle.

As we walked down the aisle, Luke kept looking at the prices of the toy cars. He kept saying, "Too expensive."

When we got back to the home, the director asked if I wanted to take Luke home for a pre-adoption visit. Of course I said, "Yes." Luke was called in and asked if he would like to spend the weekend with me at my home and visit a local historical landmark. He said, "Yes," so we hurriedly packed some clothes and took off.

It was evening, and there were several hundred miles to travel. Luke fell asleep on the front seat, and I put my hand over his shoulder. As I was driving, he asked if he could watch Bugs Bunny on TV the next morning. I said, "Yes."

When we got home, I showed him his room, and we both went to bed. The next morning, he saw my chess set and wanted to play chess. We did. When he saw pictures of me hiking across the Grand Canyon, he wanted to do that. My dream for a dad-and-son hike across the Grand Canyon seemed closer. We also toured a local historical landmark.

That afternoon, we went to meet my caseworker. While waiting in the office, I asked Luke if he wanted to change his first name. He said, "Yes." I gave him a list of first names he might like. He selected Jerry, which just so happened to be the name I had been hoping he would pick. What Luke was telling me with his new first name was that he wished to start a new life with me and break away from his past. For his middle name, he allowed me to select Wes, my dad's name. I suspect my caseworker told Luke's caseworker about the chess set (I saw her make a note of it when she visited my home), mentioned I liked Bugs Bunny, wanted to hike the Grand Canyon with my son, and the name Jerry pleased me the most.

During Luke's visit, I was so excited and anxious that I was sleeping poorly, and that caused me to be irritable. When I took him to the airport to fly back to the home, I had not gotten any sleep for two nights. After he left, I again spent another sleepless night. The inability to sleep due to extreme emotional anxiety caused me to be very irrational and delirious. I called a close friend, George, in the middle of the night. He was an old college roommate and fraternity brother of mine. The way I talked, he knew something was wrong.

He got my parents in the middle of the night and talked me into going to the hospital. It just so happened that George and I had another friend who was a resident at the hospital, who gave instructions as to how to get me into the psychiatric clinic. We got there, and there was a long wait, so we left with the intention of coming back the next morning. The next morning, my parents arranged for me to see a psychiatrist at a private psychiatric hospital.

Finally, the doctor arrived. He said he wanted to admit me for tests. I was frightened because to admit myself would mean I would lose Jerry. The doctor said that I may have a brain tumor. I went back into the admissions office to think about it. If I did not admit myself and was really mentally ill, that would be bad for Jerry. If I was mentally ill, I needed to admit myself but would lose Jerry. If I was not mentally ill, then what did I have to worry about?

I decided to admit myself. As expected, I lost Jerry. My worst nightmare became a reality. Dropping him off at the airport was the last time I saw him. My caseworker told me there were other families for him. She assured me that he would be okay.

To this day, I do not know what happened to him or where he is.

I lost Luke (Jerry), Mark, and Matt. At least I have the satisfaction of knowing I lost my boys because I acted in their best interests.

The psychiatrist misdiagnosed me and prescribed the wrong medicines for me. I was taking antipsychotic drugs, antischizophrenia drugs, and manic-depression drugs, all of which really messed my mind up. I needed the psychiatrist to find the right drugs for me.

Three months later, there was a second stay in the hospital. I flipped out at work and had to be taken back to the psychiatric hospital in an ambulance. At the hospital, I kept saying I wanted to hold Jerry in my arms. The reality of truly losing him had hit.

After the second episode, an Episcopal priest told me it is very important that psychiatrists have a strong conviction of spirituality. The priest suggested I ask my current psychiatrist if he was a Christian, which I did.

My psychiatrist's reply was, "Why do you ask?"

The Episcopal priest suggested I contact a specific psychiatrist, Dr. Joug. I asked if he was religious. He said he was Jewish. I switched psychiatrists. My family thought I was making a mistake. They believed I was denying I had a problem and was trying to place it on the first psychiatrist.

Within weeks after working with this second psychiatrist, I improved noticeably. He treated me for anxiety using relaxation and stress-management therapy. He and the therapist wanted me to take an anti-anxiety medication on an as-needed basis.

After my first experience with mind-altering drugs, I declined at first. Later, I took the anti-anxiety medication on an as-needed basis. In less then a year, I was over it. The psychiatrist wrote a letter stating he saw nothing wrong with me adopting.

I went back to the private adoption agency with the psychiatrist's letter to try again with another adoption. The agency's director said they could not work with me. I was given no explanation. For the next year, I contacted several adoption agencies and provided them with the psychiatrist's letter. All turned me down.

My first psychiatrist implied that admitting myself to a psychiatric hospital was like going in with a broken leg due to a car accident. Unfortunately, many people do *not* see it that way. Although a broken leg may fully heal, many people see mental illness as never healing. The psychiatrist's letter was ignored.

Meanwhile, though my dream of hiking across the Grand Canyon with Jerry was dead, I had pledged to myself in the psychiatric hospital that I would see to it that other dads and sons would have such an experience. At least I could come close to experiencing hiking with my son through other dads. Remembering the scout troop on my first hike at the Canyon, I decided to start with a Boy Scout troop.

For the next twenty-four years, I led five such hikes with dads and sons. The Boy Scout troop was the first and was accomplished in 1987, four years after losing Jerry.

MY QUEST TO BE A SINGLE DAD

2005 Grand Canyon group on North Rim

*2000 Hike across the Grand Canyon;
I'm fourth from left*

I decided to get more involved with Boy Scouts to improve my experience of working with boys and wait a few years before trying again to adopt and improve my disposition. My former caseworker said there needed to be time between my psychiatric episode and another attempt to adopt.

Boy Scout Troop 848

While under the care of my first psychiatrist, I went to the Boy Scout troop that Mark and I had attended. I suggested to the troop adults the idea of hiking across the Grand Canyon. I told them I would pay for the trip and that I had already hiked the Canyon three times. They thought such a trip was too much and proposed instead a backpacking trip within the state. I went with their suggestion. We went on a backpack campout to a place where I had backpacked before: the basin at Big Bend National Park.

Setting up camp at Big Bend National Park before backpack hike

While out on the hike at Big Bend, there was a problem with the scoutmaster. I kept telling him the boys needed their packs to be as light as possible and that they needed to leave their dirty laundry and other nonessentials with the cars. But the scoutmaster insisted that the boys were to be self-contained and carry everything they had. I knew the boys would have problems. However, what was I to say or do? I was just another adult leader with no scouting troop training. And I was under psychiatric care.

Hiking up the mountain out of the Basin, many boys started to have problems. I urged them to pace according to their breathing, stop and rest until breathing returned to normal. The adults ignored that, since it slowed the group down too much, and insisted that everyone hike together at the same pace. This was getting me upset. The adults were ignoring the limits of the boys, who were only ages eleven to fourteen.

I suggested that I take three boys to move ahead and start setting up camp. That way, the rest of the troop could slow down and not worry about getting the campsite set up. The three boys and I followed my rules for pacing by breathing, and we arrived at the campsite in good shape. After we set up camp, I ran down the trail and found all the adults resting. They could not believe how I had been able to carry a pack and still not be tired. The adults told me two boys had collapsed on the trail and could no longer carry their packs. The adults had to carry their packs for them. The next morning, the scoutmaster admitted that the boys' packs had been too heavy.

Hiking down the mountain was easier, but the two slowest boys, Tom and Tim, were put in front of the group to encourage them to move faster. I was up front with them and kept trying to allow them to rest. But all the other boys and adults ridiculed them and yelled at them to keep going. All I could do was stop when they stopped and say it was okay. I tried to hold up the troop as long as I could until the adults started to complain.

The adults did not follow my rules for breathing and failed to listen to how the boys were breathing. When you are gasping for breath, you need to stop and rest. Yelling at them will do nothing. I should have pulled the adults aside and told them that different boys have different physical limits. Yelling at them will not improve their true physical limits. I would have reminded them how two boys had collapsed on the trail the day before and that I had never ridiculed them for not keeping up with me when we hiked up the mountain.

After that campout, Tom and Tim dropped out

of scouting. Looking back, I realized I should have stepped in and done something, but I was under psychiatric care and on medication. Emotionally and mentally, I was not able to put my foot down.

Wood Badge

About a year later, I heard about Wood Badge training at an adult scout training session. My caseworker with Jerry (Luke) had told me to get involved in scouting and take Wood Badge training. She implied that it could help me prepare to be a better parent. Wood Badge training was being touted as a way to establish order in a chaotic meeting. Graduates of Wood Badge said you could get the boys to run their own meetings and make their own decisions. I didn't believe it until I did it myself.

Right after completing a year of psychotherapy, I enrolled in a Wood Badge course. It was in the spring. I still remember the Bluebonnet flowers in our parade field. At a meal during the Wood Badge course, my group was talking and kidding around. One group member said something about being crazy. I said I was the crazy one in the group, and I had papers to prove it. They all looked at me funny. What was I saying? Later, I told them about my psychiatric experience. The group leader later told me that they were very surprised to hear I'd had mental problems. Had I not told them, they would never have known.

My tent mate was a young man who told me he had been in a children's home from age four to age eleven because his parents had been unable to care for him. They still kept in contact with him at the children's home. One day, a staff member had come into his room and told him he was going home to his family. He told me he was shocked because virtually all he knew was a children's home. That really hit me. Here I was hoping to adopt, and I was sharing a tent with someone who, as a child, had lived in a children's home wondering if he would ever go home.

My Wood Badge ticket (applied project) was at first to take a scout troop on a hike across the Grand Canyon. But my Wood Badge adviser told me that was too much. My ticket had to be completed within two years. He strongly suggested I teach others how to do such a hike. I changed my ticket to teaching scout leaders how to do the hike.

At a Wood Badge meeting, the course director said we would apply the leadership skills we learned "without thinking." This course programmed me to be a leader of boys. Wood Badge is a course *all* parents should take. It is a great course to learn how to manage boys and adults in scouting, provided you have the right attitude.

Scout Summer Camp

The summer after the Wood Badge course, I was the business manager at a scout camp. It was a great experience and follow-up to Wood Badge. During the seven weeks there, I was able to teach scout leaders how to hike the Grand Canyon.

As an adult staff member, you are working from the time you get up in the morning until the time you go to bed in the evening. Even at meals, I had to help in the kitchen and supervise kids at the tables.

What a great experience! Yes, I survived seven weeks of living with hundreds of kids ages eleven to sixteen.

Scouts on a backpack trip at summer camp

Building a monkey bridge at summer camp

The last week of summer camp, I was inducted into the Order of the Arrow (OA), a scout honor fraternal order. It recognizes those who put the needs of others before their own. I was inducted due to my work at the scout camp. Right after the campfire where I was inducted, we started the induction campout, called an Ordeal. Immediately, I was taken to a brief ritual to prepare the candidates to sleep alone under the stars. While I was getting set for the first time in my life, it seemed as if I was being prepared for something beyond my imagination. During the induction rituals for that weekend, we learned service to others by putting our needs aside. Later, we learned in the brotherhood ceremony never to give burdens to others. These ideals of the OA are things my sons need to learn from me and hopefully from the OA.

Getting into Troop 848

After summer camp I returned to the troop I had taken backpacking at Big Bend National Park. There was a new, untrained scoutmaster, one of the adults who had been ridiculing the two slow boys on the backpacking trip.

When the new scoutmaster saw I was a member of the Order of the Arrow, he said, "I see you are a member of the Order of the Assholes."

I told him I had an opportunity to be a scoutmaster for a troop north of town and politely left, never to return. I remember looking back at the boys playing as I walked away. I knew they would be okay. Their dads were involved with them.

That troop north of town was really very iffy. I had heard about it as a side comment from a scout leader at summer camp. I had only said it to make a polite exit. I contacted a friend from my Wood Badge group and asked if he knew of a troop needing a Wood-Badge-trained adult. He invited me to his troop, 848. I was hesitant to go since they already had several trained adults. The scoutmaster was Wood Badge along with my friend, who was his assistant. Would they need another Wood Badge adult?

When I arrived at my first Troop 848 meeting, I noticed this troop was operating like a troop should. The boys were running their meeting without any adults. The scoutmaster and other adults were in the back doing other things. Scoutmaster Frank Fox was very friendly and invited me to join them on a campout. I was happy and worried. I was single, had never been married, had a history of mental illness, and wanted to work with the kids on campouts. Would the parents trust me with their sons?

On that first campout, Frank and I shared the same tent. I felt that this was a good time to tell him about my psychiatric past. He needed to know in case I flipped out again. He had a right to know. I told him about my desire to adopt. I also told him that after completing a year of therapy, Wood Badge had programmed me to be a leader of boys. As Frank put it, therapy had made me a blank slate, and the course had reprogrammed me. To my surprise, Frank thanked me for sharing my past with him.

I joined Troop 848. Frank put me in charge of all the parents and adults to help lead the troop committee of parents and be in charge of the adults on campouts. I really wanted to work with the boys, but I did what I was told to do. After a few months, I started to work with the boys. It finally resulted in me becoming second in command after Frank. This gave me great confidence with dealing with a group of boys and their parents.

At an Order of the Arrow induction campout (an Ordeal), Frank and I were supervising the candidates, hanging out with them while they waited for dinner in silence. While sitting there, Frank leaned over to me and asked, "Why have you not put your paperwork in for the Scouter's Leadership Award? You have completed all the requirements."

I replied, "That award is just a piece of cloth. I have no desire to show off how great I am. I did those things for the kids. My reward and only interest are enhancing the growth and maturity of young men."

He leaned back in his chair and said, "I understand. Do it anyway. It will give you credibility in the things you do and will inspire others."

At the next Court of Honor, I received the Scouter's Leadership Award.

During another scouting event, an adult leader was trying to get me to go to Philmont, the national scout camp. He said that to be a true adult scout leader, you must go to Philmont.

My reply: "A true adult scout leader is one who enhances the growth and maturity of young men."

Campout Number One—Solve Problems

A goal in scouting is to teach the boys how to solve problems. When the boys asked me to help them set up their tents, I said, "Look at my tent and see how I set it up. Then go back and try again. If you still have problems, come get me."

The boys were able to set up their tents without my help. Once, a few boys needed a pitcher to make Kool-Aid. I told them the adults did not have an extra pitcher. I asked what they were going to do. They thought for a moment and said they would put a little Kool-Aid in each cup and mix it. Scouts can solve their own problems when given the guidance and opportunity to do so.

Campout Number Two—Not be a Burden on Others

On another campout, a group of boys forgot to bring their dinner. They asked me if the adults had any extra food. I said, "No," and instructed them to go back to their tents and plan a skit for the campfire. They had to learn about responsibility and the consequences of forgetting and not to be a burden to others.

I also told them to remember that after the campfire there would be a cracker barrel by the adults. We adults would be providing all the boys with fruit, cheese, and crackers before they went to bed. They didn't go to bed hungry, and they learned a lesson about responsibility and consequence.

Campout Number Three—What the Boy Scouts Learned

On one campout, we went to Lost Maples State Park and backpacked into the forest about two miles. I was the lead adult in charge of the campout. On the drive there, the older boy leaders were in my car. As I drove, I asked them to develop a plan for the weekend. What games were they going to play, and what program skills were they to work on? They all wanted to play Capture the Flag and do something with first aid. I suggested they teach the younger boys first aid in the morning and play Capture the Flag in the afternoon. During the game, they could have one of the older boys pretend to fall and break his leg. The adults could be hiding in the bushes. The older kids loved it and started talking and planning the first aid skills and game. One of the older kids, Steve, said he would pretend to break his leg.

The next morning Steve and the others taught the younger boys first aid. After lunch they went down to some rocks on the creek to play Capture the Flag. We adults hid in the bushes. One adult ran down the trail and hid; his job was to stop any of the boys from going for the park ranger. We could hear and see the kids play. Suddenly, Steve fell and yelled out. All the other kids gathered around.

Result: they panicked. There was confusion and excitement. One boy ran back to camp to get us and was yelling for us. He ran back and told the others he could not find the adults and was almost crying. Panic increased.

Finally, Steve got up and smiled, and the adults emerged from the bushes. We all went back to camp. The younger kids were still very excited about the experience. I asked them what they had learned. They were still hyper and could not think. Finally, I told them that in an emergency, first aid skills, which they had learned that morning, are useless if you panic.

Campout Number Four—How to Stop Two Boys' Fighting

On another campout I led, we had two boys who were constantly fighting, Bill and Bob. When we arrived at the campsite, these two got in a real fistfight. The boy leader, Jack, and I also got some hits as we pulled them apart. I told them to go to their tents and stay there until campfire. At campfire, there was verbal aggression between the two. I told them to stop and made sure they were separated.

The next morning, after we all got a good night's sleep, Bill and Bob had cooled off. I asked each of them who in the troop they felt most comfortable with and trusted. I got those two other scouts and Jack and took the five kids off to a tree. I sat Bill, Bob, their two trusted friends, and Jack up against the tree. Bill and Bob were seated next to each other and facing the other three.

I told the two trusted friends and Jack, "These two, Bill and Bob, have been fighting like cats and dogs. Last night's fistfight was unacceptable. You are to decide who is guilty and who is innocent. Then decide on punishment for the guilty one. Punishment can be anything except expulsion from the troop. You may recommend that to the adults."

I walked away. From a distance, I kept an eye on the five under that tree. After twenty minutes, they all got up and walked away. Later, Jack told me that it had just been a misunderstanding. All was well. For the rest of the campout, they worked together. Problem solved. Kids can handle kid problems better than adults. I knew Jack would fix things. His father was a minister.

Campout Number Five—How to Deal with a Hyperactive Teenager

At an OA campout, Paul, a hyperactive fifteen-year-old, was eating dinner in the dining hall. Paul was loud and unruly. Finally, I had the kid sitting next to Paul move. I sat next to Paul and whispered into his ear with a soft voice, "Look around. How many other boys are acting the way you are?"

Paul said his dad had told him he was hyper. For the next twenty to thirty minutes he was normal. Then he started being hyper and loud again but to a lesser degree. Maybe whispering in the ear of a hyperactive child every twenty to thirty minutes is better than medication.

Grand Canyon Goal Realized

In 1987, four years after I set my goal at the psychiatric hospital and two years after I wrote my Wood Badge ticket, I took twelve Scouts and six adults on a hike across the Grand Canyon. There were three father-son groups. This was a very complex trip: two weeks, several thousand miles, and six cars. The older boys wanted to follow another adult. I stepped back and let the other adult work with the teenagers. Lesson from Wood Badge: Share leadership and use the expertise of group members.

Scouts at Cottonwood ranger station, Grand Canyon, AZ

*Scouts at Colorado River, Grand Canyon;
Mule bridge in background*

There was one incident where I did put my foot down. When we arrived at the bottom of the Grand Canyon, all the adults and boys wanted to do another six miles to complete the twenty-mile hiking merit badge requirement.

I said firmly, "You just hiked fourteen miles to the bottom of the Grand Canyon with temperatures exceeding 120 degrees. You have no idea what the heat has done to your body. I have done this three times."

They did not listen. They were going to do the extra six miles without me. Although I wanted to rest and take it easy, I went with them since I was responsible for the trip. When the group got to a fork in the trail, they all looked at me as to which way to go. I pointed in the direction that was easier, following the river. The other route would have involved uphill hiking out of the inner gorge. After about a mile, boys started to drop. So I pulled a trick.

"Hey, how about stopping for a moment to rest, and I'll show you how to make a Polaris compass," I shouted.

It was night, and the North Star was out. All gathered around to see how to make a Polaris compass. When finished, the boys started to complain. One adult leader admitted they had made a mistake and all wanted the fastest way back to camp. I said to go back the way we had come.

That trip did take a toll on me. Yes, I fulfilled a goal I had set in the psychiatric hospital. But the emptiness of lacking a son on that Grand Canyon trip hurt even more than before. I was still grieving for Jerry. When we got back home, the kids returned to their parents, and I returned to an empty house, where I cried. I started to feel that being an assistant scoutmaster was not my calling, yet I wanted to continue in scouting.

The following year I left Troop 848 because of a new job two hundred miles away. Before I left, Frank Fox noticed I was anxious. He suggested I become the district training chairman at my new location. Frank pointed out that I would teach other parents how to be good scout leaders, make good contacts, and know which were the best units in the district. It sounded like a good idea.

Boy Scout Troop YCF: Bad Boys in Prison

While on the district committee at my new job location, I learned there was a troop at a youth correctional facility (YCF), a kids' prison. I contacted the facility to see if I could work with the troop. The director told me that first I had to get a criminal background check. No problem with that. And I had to take a psychological evaluation. That could be a problem. I was afraid of failing it but decided to take it anyway, if only to learn how I was doing. Maybe, just maybe, I would indeed pass and the YCF would allow me to work with these kids.

The psychological evaluation was the MMPI, 550 true-false questions. It is designed to detect any psychopathologies and deceptions. About a week after I took the MMPI, the director called me to tell me about the training and orientation for volunteers at the facility. I asked about my psychological exam. She said I had passed. I wanted to talk to the facility psychologist to make sure. The psychologist told me all scales were well within normal limits. What a pleasant surprise!

At the first training and orientation for YCF volunteers, a fifteen-year-old male student was brought in. The kids in the facility were always referred to as *students*. He appeared to be very depressed, lonely, and eager for adult attention.

The next orientation meeting, we toured the facility. We walked by the little boys' dorm for ages eleven to thirteen. The name of the recreation hall was something I'll always remember: the Getaway. I found that building name very interesting because all the students had a desire to get away *from* the facility.

We passed the communication building, where students' locations were monitored and recorded. It was also the building for solitary confinement. When a student was taken to communication, they were given slippers, short pants, and a t-shirt. They had to write why they were sent to communication and how they felt. Each room had only a bed, table, chair, and secured window. To get to that room, you had to go through three locked doors.

Students could also be locked up in the YCF vehicles. The back window knob and door opener of YCF vehicles were disabled. If they were on a field trip off the facility and there was a problem, the back part of the vehicle was a secure place to hold the student. Most of the vehicles had no YCF markings.

If we went on a field trip, no one knew where these students had come from.

At another training session, we were told that some of the students were former sex slaves to predators. These were street kids, runaways, and tortured victims. We had to be very careful about touching them and expect to receive a fight-or-flight reaction.

As I was going through training and orientation, everything seemed familiar to me. *Matt!* Most of what I saw and heard reminded me of Matt. Was this the treatment facility Matt had told me about? If I ever meet Matt again, this will be one of my first questions to him.

For five years, I was the assistant scoutmaster for that troop. I learned a lot from that experience, for example, *shadowing*. When a student was having a problem, he must shadow one of the staff members. The student must stand near and follow a staff member. He must always be within one arm's length of the staff member.

Another method was that after school, the students would walk back to the dorm in silence with hands behind their backs and stay in their rooms for fifteen to twenty minutes. This was to get them to settle down after school.

Entering buildings was also very structured. When the scouts reached the recreation hall, where we held meetings, they lined up against the wall on the porch in silence. Staff member one would open the door. Staff member two walked in. Then the scouts walked in behind staff member two with staff member one still at the door, watching both inside and outside. These kids were emotionally unstable. Structure and routine were designed to keep stimulation and excitement to a minimum.

I learned what *lockdown* meant and why it was used. One day, when I arrived for a troop meeting, the recreation director told me the facility was on lockdown. All the students were locked in their rooms, and the staff was interrogating the students one at a time. A knife was missing from the kitchen. I thought it sad that so many had to suffer punishment for the actions of one or two students. The recreation director pointed out that lockdown was to protect the students and prevent one student from knifing another.

I learned a lot about the need for structure and routine when dealing with troubled youth. The scouts at the YCF taught me always to consider the *why* of a student's behavior. I learned that for some, consequences are the only things that keep them from bad behavior. One of the scouts told me he saw absolutely nothing wrong with stealing from stores, but he would not steal because he did not want to return to YCF.

Another technique used on these students was *put on floor*. In all my years at YCF, I never saw it done in the troop. It did happen in the dorms and school. When a student blew up, the staff gently held the student on the floor until he settled down or communication staff arrived.

Of all the troops I worked with, this was the best.

There was little advancement and no campouts, but the boys always looked out for one another. Every boy was part of the group, unless he was in communication. It helped me understand why Grandpa loved the kids at the Oregon YCF.

There are three experiences that stand out in my mind.

YCF Experience Number One

The YCF Scouts were never allowed to do any overnight campouts. The risks of escape or fight were too high. Control over them was very low. Staff would have to be up all night watching as the scouts slept. Instead, one summer, I arranged for them to visit a scout summer camp for a day. The plan was to have a picnic, fish, and hike.

When we arrived at our picnic site, the scoutmaster and I got out and opened the back doors of the vehicle to let the scouts out. We were near the camp cooking program area. One of the teenage scout staff members came over to us and invited us to visit his program area. The staff member had no idea who my scouts were. They could have been murderers, pimps, drug pushers, thieves, sex offenders, and muggers. That scout showed us how to do some camp cooking and gave us some samples of the demonstration. We all had a very enjoyable visit at that program area.

After lunch, some of the scouts wanted to go fishing, and I took three around to visit the other program areas. We even visited two campsites and met other scouts and adult leaders. At each program area, the youth staff welcomed us and showed us the scout skills of that area.

When we got back to our YCF van, one of the scouts told me that this was the first time he'd felt like a normal kid since being placed in the YCF. Everyone treated him as if he were just another kid at summer camp. For about an hour, he'd had the sensation of being a normal kid, but that short hour had a lifelong positive effect. This boy reached tenure in the scouting program.

YCF Experience Number Two

Once a week, I would meet the scoutmaster in the recreation office. We would walk over to the school and enter from the back door. We would have the scouts line up outside, hands behind their backs, and march in silence to the Getaway. One time, as soon as I walked into the entry area of the school from the back, all the scouts rushed around me and blocked my path. They said something like, "Did you hear Joe got paroled? What are we going to do today? Can we go fishing next meeting?"

They were pouring it on thick, I noticed. The scoutmaster sat over to the side and talked quietly with another staff member. While these ever-so-charming scouts were keeping me occupied, I saw across the room a twelve- or thirteen-year-old boy next to the front door. He was leaning against the wall, arms folded, staring into space. Other students and staff kept a distance from him. Then some communication staff came through the front door. The staff handcuffed the boy's hands behind his back and took him away to communication. What these scouts did was very honorable. They kept me away from the troubled boy in a polite way. They were protecting both the boy and me from further problems.

YCF Experience Number Three

This experience is the one most meaningful to me. It involves a YCF scout I'll call John. At the age of eleven, he walked into his classroom, pulled out a gun, and shot his teacher, an adult male authority figure. Had the teacher died and had John been ten years older, he would have been on death row. John reminded me of my dad's story of seeing a fifteen-year-old murderer at the Oregon YCF my grandpa had worked at.

Before entering YCF, John had been an active scout. When he joined our troop, he was quite interested in earning merit badges. He had been working toward his first-class rank when he had shot his teacher. His problem was a father who beat him severely as punishment for failure.

The first merit badge we worked on was Citizenship in the Nation. I'll never forget the first time I was alone with him in a locked room to which I did not have the key. I did have the pen because a pen can be a dangerous weapon in the wrong hands.

As we began, John started to get very agitated.

I saw the anger and fear in his eyes. He was ready to blow, no staff around, and I was a male adult authority figure like his teacher. You might think I was scared. I was not. In fact, I was really enjoying this session with him. I knew why he had shot his teacher... fear of failure.

Immediately I said, "Look, if you mess up, I'll go over it with you, and I will be back next week to try again." I repeated that several times, and he settled down immediately. What surprised me was that he calmed down in a few seconds. Usually, such emotional arousal takes ten to fifteen minutes to calm down. He finished the merit badge in two meetings.

John was the most lovable kid at YCF. If I had had the chance, I would have loved to take him home. He was the type of child anyone would love to have as a son, even if he did shoot his teacher with a gun. Just remove the fear and abuse, and you have an Eagle Scout. He did express to me an interest in pursuing the Eagle rank.

After two years at YCF, John was paroled. His mother remarried, and the family moved out of state. Before he left, I got him all his scouting documents showing that he was finally at first class rank with a few merit badges. If he wanted to work toward Eagle, he would have the paperwork.

I tried to make sure there was nothing in his scout paperwork to indicate he had been at YCF. My goal was to give him a good cover story. When someone asked about this time period of his life, he could say he was in the Scouts working toward Eagle.

I know for a fact that he did advance to the next rank. I hope he changed his last name to that of his stepfather. That will help him break away from the past. Although I could have tried to contact him after he left YCF, I didn't. John deserved a new start on life.

Try Every Five Years for Twenty-Four Years

Starting in 1983–1984, approximately every five years or so, for the next twenty-four years, I improved my situation by getting more education and relocating for a better job. At each new start, I tried CPS and other private adoption agencies. Here is my try, try, try, try, try, and try again story.

Try Again: 1989

Five years after my first attempt to adopt, following my hospitalization, I tried a second time. I had a new job and new location in northeast Texas, a fresh start. Also, I was getting into the scouting program at the district level and at a youth correctional faculty.

I thought I would try a private agency this time. A religious agency accepted my application. I'll call this Agency Number One. I met once with the caseworker. At that first meeting, I told her about my mental past. The next meeting was at my home. There, the caseworker and her supervisor told me they would not work with me. My mental past seemed to be a factor in their decision.

The next year I tried another private agency that I'll call Agency Number Two. I told them about the religious agency that had turned me down and about my mental history. They talked to my psychologist, who worked with me for one year after my hospitalization, and a current therapist. The therapist told this private agency he believed I would be a good parent to an adoptive child.

The psychological evaluation by the therapist said I had persevered to adopt in the face of adverse circumstances and that my psychological status appeared to have been somewhat overblown at the time. I was stable and doing quite well. Since I had been stable for six years, there was a good prognosis, although I had more difficulty in expressing feelings than most individuals. The psychological evaluation indicated I was free of any psychopathology and was working on some issues. The evaluation by the therapist recommended proceeding with adoption with care and planning. I was best suited for a passive type of child and needed to learn more about adoption risks. With this information, the private agency approved my home study for a domestic adoption.

All was going well until the director of the religious Agency Number One met the director of private Agency Number Two. The director of Agency Number One told the other director that her agency had done a home study on me. The director of Agency Number Two thought this meant I had lied on my application when I indicated that there was no recent home study done by another agency. My response was that if Agency Number One had done a home study, where was the document? I had already told my caseworker that I had gone to Agency Number One, but they had turned me down. Director number two agreed there was a problem with semantics but decided to close my file anyway.

The following year, I tried the state's Child Protective Services again. The state agency accepted me for foster/adopt training and orientation. An issue that came up during the sessions was why I had not talked about my mental history during the sessions with the other people in training. My response was that not everyone would be sympathetic and understanding, and I had the right to be careful about what I said and to whom.

The caseworkers kept telling me that the children they had would not fit me. Their problems were too severe for me to handle. Yet on the web adoption listing, I found several boys up for adoption who had mild emotional disturbances or none at all. There were kids out there who would fit me, just very few. Eventually, in 1992, I was called into the agency's office to be told they would not work with me. They insisted that none of the children available were suited for me.

Try Again: 1994

My third try was in 1994. I had another new job and another new location in north central Texas, another fresh start. When I started the training again for foster/adopt by Child Protective Services, I learned that the 1983 agency that had worked with me on a placement with Luke from CPS no longer had any file on me. The explanation given to me was that for a private agency, if a placement does not occur, the home study or file is destroyed after five years. However, all CPS records are kept.

Child Protective Services wanted another psychological assessment. The assessment indicated that I had an anxiety disorder that was in remission. I was able to read red flags and knew how to deal with the anxiety. The report stated I can function at a high level and in a controlled manner under most circumstances. It appeared that Child Protective Services was again going to close my file. To avoid another recorded denial by CPS, I requested that my file be closed, and it was.

Since adoption was out again, I decided in 1997 to pursue a PhD after the offer of a teaching job while I pursued my doctorate in computer education. So I was starting over again at a university in Texas.

Try Again: 2001

In 2001 I received my doctorate. My job was rewarding and provided me a lot of flexibility in work hours. In my early fifties, I decided to try again—this time with the aid of a licensed family therapist. My sessions with him were to make sure I was ready for an adoption and have him ready for family counseling should a placement occur.

My thinking was that the day after placement, we would start family counseling. Better to fix a problem before it got worse. Too many times, families—especially adoption families—start getting help only after a problem has already developed. Many times, parents see the problem as something that pertains only to the child. My opinion is that family counseling is a team effort. I as the parent need to be part of the counseling with my child. I may need it too.

Finally, after getting the okay from the therapist, I applied to Child Protective Services again. There was nothing to lose. Again, I was in training and orientation.

My therapist wrote, "I believe the patient is viable as a prospect as an adoptive parent. I do not feel these issues will affect his ability to make a careful and thoughtful home for a child. My recommendation would be that you give him a chance in some way to prove himself."

During that training, I learned that when a child was up for adoption, the caseworker gathered five home studies. At a meeting of CPS staff, one of the five home studies would be selected for placement. In other words, I would be competing with four other families. The caseworkers chose the family. The family did not choose the child. If a child was found who fit me *and* a two-parent family, the two-parent family would get priority.

A question I posed to the caseworker during a training session was, "Why are foster children moved from foster home to foster home so often?"

He said he did not know. How could he not know? He himself made decisions about moving children from one foster home to the next. The answer was something most caseworkers do not want the public to know. Many times, the child's problems exceed what the foster family can deal with.

At the last session of training, an adoptive family was brought in. The adoptive mother told how their teenage adopted son was hyperactive, attention deficient, and a victim of fetal alcohol syndrome. His birth mother had been an alcoholic during pregnancy. He had two younger brothers who had been adopted by another family. A few weeks after this teenager was placed with this adoptive family, he had received a letter from one of his younger brothers. It stated the younger brother did not want to have anything to do with him and to stay out of his life. The teenager was devastated.

A few years later, the teenager got a phone call from this younger brother. The younger brother had just run away from home. When they got together that same evening, the teenager found out that this younger brother did not send that letter. It was from the adoptive mother. It seems that the placement of the younger brothers had problems over the years. Considering the attitude of the adoptive mother with that letter to the older teenage brother, it is understandable why the placement went bad. I asked if the adoptive parents of his younger brothers had forced them to change their first names. The answer was yes. I suspect the adoptive mother wanted this older brother out of the picture with the two adoptive younger brothers, a complete and permanent break. The fact that the first names of the two younger brothers were forcefully changed by the parents suggests to me the parents were domineering and had a need to control.

After ten weeks of waiting for the CPS caseworker to receive my past files, he called me into his office. He told me the kids they had would not fit me. Again I pointed out kids who would, based on information I had gathered from the Web listings. He said I was unable to deal with that type of child. My failure with Mark had proved that. My response was that I had been able to deal with Mark longer than two two-parent families and that Mark had required residential treatment. His problems had exceeded what two two-parent families could handle. I had been able to deal with him longer and had kept in touch with him after he left, where the other two-parent families had not.

My contention was that the experience with Mark proved I was just as good as or better than two two-parent foster families. The caseworker replied that since it had occurred more than twenty years ago, it no longer applied. I should have asked why he'd brought it up in the first place. Sometimes your best lines occur to you after you have made your speech. My position was that if whatever had happened twenty years ago no longer applied, he should also have disregarded my psychiatric hospitalization twenty years ago.

    I appealed to his supervisor. She supported his decision. I appealed to the CPS regional director. She finally allowed a home study, which rejected me, again. To bring my trials with CPS to an end, the director gave me an honorable exit. She acknowledged that I had sought counseling and support dealing with adoption issues, and I pledged that I would get into family counseling immediately when a placement occurred. She told me I should go with a private agency that places from out-of-state. There would be more opportunities to find a child who fits me, she said.

    Since my relationship with CPS was over, I decided to look at private agencies for either domestic or international adoption. Around 2002, I met a family in scouting who had adopted a Russian girl and boy. Since I'd had so much trouble with the domestic adoption system, and I had a good-paying job, international adoption from Russia or the Ukraine became a possibility.

    I visited one private international agency. When I asked the director if her agency was accredited by Russia, she said, "Yes." That was an outright lie. It pays to do your homework and research the facts first. It also pays to appear ignorant. When I asked why her agency was not listed on the Russian Embassy

Web site nor on the American Moscow Embassy Web site as accredited, she replied that to get accredited the agency has to have a number of placements first and they were working on that. Another lie! You get accredited by obeying Russian laws and providing follow-up reports after placement. Agencies have to show that follow-up.

After talking with her more, I learned that her agency really did independent placements through a Russian lawyer. When she told me she could not provide references, I ended the conversation. Later I checked the Better Business Bureau and found out there were complaints against this agency.

When I contacted several international adoption agencies, I soon learned that most did not accept single men because the country did not accept single men. Some international agencies were dishonest. One agency said the Ukraine did not accept single men. I had an e-mail from the Ukrainian Embassy in Washington, D.C., that stated the Ukraine did accept single men.

Unfortunately, the truth is that almost all international adoption agencies only accepted single women. But I kept trying until I found a private agency that would work with me.

Try Again: 2002—Private Agency Rimstone Adoptions—Domestic Again

In 2002, I contacted an agency I'll call Rimstone Adoption Agency. They had an international program with Russia. Like the other agencies, they did not work with single men. But the staff member said that their domestic program would accept single men. So I decided to try Rimstone's domestic adoption and do an out-of-state placement instead of international.

During training and orientation with Rimstone, we discussed changing an older child's first name. Should the first name be changed to break away from the past? Or should the child keep the first name so as to keep continuity with self-identity? Many parents want to give a new first name to an older child, thinking that it will help give a new start in life. However, some children may want to keep their birth names because they want to keep a link to their pasts.

When this question was posed, my reply was simply, "Whatever the child feels most comfortable with."

After that session, one attendee told me that I would make a great dad.

Part of the training included visiting a therapeutic foster home, which helps children with severe problems beyond what a basic foster home can provide. There I learned that love and understanding alone are not always enough. The therapeutic foster parents adopted a boy with extremely severe problems. As the mother put it, she had to consider the neighbors. What if this boy killed the neighbors' pet or set fire to the neighbors' house? She told me that things looked bad. She and her husband, therapeutic foster parents who took severe cases, would be going to court to nullify the adoption and return this boy to the state. Luckily, they found a psychiatrist who prescribed an antipsychotic aggression medication. It worked. The adoption was saved by a pill.

When the training was over, the caseworker visited my home. I knew that within a few seconds of her arrival, I would know if I was approved. After all of these tries and home visits, I can tell if the caseworker is accepting of me. Touring the apartment, she saw the second bedroom with two beds and the second bathroom. She was impressed with the river and park near my home. I suspected that I had passed inspection, and it turned out I was right. The approval stipulated that I keep a daily log for the first six months, attend continuing education classes, have frequent visits by the caseworker for the first three months, and be paired with a foster parent mentor.

For eight months, only a few children were presented to me. Most did not fit. The few who did fit, other families were considered. Remember, a couple has priority over a single man, and I was one of five families being considered for each child. I soon realized that Rimstone Adoption Agency was contracted with CPS. In other words, I was only being considered for children within the state, not out-of-state as I first thought. About six months after approval, the caseworker wanted me to be just a foster home and to forget adopting for now. I realized that this was not working. So I started to look into international adoption again.

Try Again Internationally

Early 2004: Rimstone International Adoption Agency

The more I looked into international adoption, the more I felt that this was for me. I felt best able to deal with the problems that led to children being in Eastern European orphanages. I suggest Google for Ukraine Orphanage 12 (http://www.orphanage.kiev.ua/) in Kiev. That Web site gives you a good idea of the daily life and schedule of one of the better orphanages in Eastern Europe. Rural orphanages are not as well off.

When I read about institutional autism, sensory integration disorder, developmental delay, and the general characteristics of Eastern European orphans, I knew that was the type of child I could help the most. I found the type of child who would be my son. And I remembered the Boy Scout I met who, at the age of eleven, had been adopted from Russia.

In early 2004, I found an agency in Washington that worked in the Ukraine. The agency's director said my domestic home study from Rimstone Adoption Agency was acceptable, but it needed to be rewritten for international. When I told my Rimstone domestic caseworker my plans to go international and that I needed an international home study, she insisted I talk to their Russian program director. When I pointed out that the last time I had checked with Rimstone's Russian program they had not accepted single men, the caseworker said I should talk to the international program director anyway.

When I met the program director, she talked me out of using the agency in Washington State and discouraged me from working with the Ukraine. She mentioned the nuclear reactor disaster in Chernobyl and said some of the children may have medical problems due to the radiation. Looking back, from all my research on adoption from the Ukraine, I found nothing to support that. In fact, I had communicated with several single men who adopted from the Ukraine, and they were pleased with the experience.

The Rimstone director also told me there were other problems with placements from the Ukraine, especially with independent adoptions (meaning work only through a facilitator in the Ukraine and not with any international agency). The bottom line is that she talked me into using their Russian program instead of going to another agency.

When I asked why they did not work with single men, she said, "If you cannot trust a Catholic priest, who can you trust?" The director was referring to a recent sex scandal that had been in the news. But she told me that if my domestic caseworker said to consider me, she would.

As soon as I said yes to use Rimstone for Russia, the director brought me a form to fill out to get things moving. As I filled out the form, the director told me to mark married where it asked if I was single. The director told me my file would be processed faster. She said that since my home study stated I am single, immigration would know that. I thought about that and proceeded anyway to mark "never married." Looking back, I should have seen the red flags here, but I was very excited about adopting from Russia.

On the back of the form, it asked how many children I wished to adopt. I told the director my domestic home study was for two and that I would eventually like to have three sons. My dream is for a sibling group. Considering the stress that international adoptive children experience, such a sibling group can provide a good support group for one another. The children would have others with the same history and experiences of being in an orphanage and later being adopted. But I knew that three might be too many to start. I better adopt two and consider a third at a later time.

However, the director said to indicate four children. I looked at her with surprise and said I felt three should be my maximum. The director said to put down four to keep all options open, so that's what I did. After I filled out the form, the director urged me to send it off quickly to get things moving, and that is what I did. I trusted her. A person in such a position would never lie or mislead a client, right?

A caseworker was assigned to me and did a home study. The home study disapproved me, the main issue being my history of mental illness, even though it was several years past. Most of the negative comments were based on the "impressions" of the caseworker. The caseworker ignored the conclusions, opinions, and recommendations from two licensed mental health practitioners. The home study lacked any psychological assessment. My therapist stated I had a mild case of Asperger's Syndrome. As my therapist put it, I was a computer nerd. Well, with a PhD in computer education, I guess so. My perception of the syndrome is that such a person thinks so much and forgets how to laugh. Well, I guess I am guilty of thinking too much, but I sure do remember how to laugh.

Although my therapist indicated that I would make a good parent, the caseworker only focused on the Asperger's Syndrome and ignored the therapist's conclusions and recommendations. She also ignored a letter from the attending psychiatrist, dated 1984, indicating there was no reason to deny me the opportunity to adopt. The caseworker's argument was that there had been no formal report or details about my illness at the time of my diagnosis and treatment. Even though the therapist, whom I worked with for more than five years, said that illness was resolved, the caseworker said the therapist had not been involved in the treatment and diagnoses.

I was devastated. That home study was so harsh; I would never be permitted to adopt internationally. My therapist suggested I check to see if I could go back to foster/adopt. When I did, Rimstone said they would work with me, but only as a domestic foster home, no adoption.

This is not what I wanted. I wanted to be a dad to my son or sons, not someone else's son who would leave after a year or so. I yearned for the lifelong commitment of adoption. I tried to find yet another private agency to do an international home study and a placement from Eastern Europe.

Late 2004: Agency Parent Maker and Immigration

There I was, a single man with an international home study of denial and a history of mental illness, who had been rejected many times by many agencies. I wasn't ready to give up. No true dad would ever give up trying to bring his sons home. What was I going to do?

Finally, after contacting several private adoption agencies, I found an agency that I'll call Parent Maker. However, Parent Maker only did home studies. When I visited the director for the first time,

I explained all the problems I had and was almost crying. After contacting my therapist, the director agreed to have an international home study done. When the caseworker visited my home, she asked several questions.

One question was what I would do if my son did not want to hike across the Grand Canyon. My response was that there were many other things we could do at the Grand Canyon as a father and son. There was the chairlift up Mount San Francisco, where I had made my decision about Mark; Lowell Observatory, where the planet Pluto was discovered; Sunset Crater; and Indian ruins. I'd rather have quality time with my son on the Grand Canyon rims than to hike across without him. In other words, my son would be more important to me than hiking the Grand Canyon.

Another question was what I would do if my son was great in the orphanage but a real problem at home. I responded that I would implement orphanage structure and routines, which I already had plans to do. In fact, I anticipated people would criticize me for treating my son as if he was still in an institution like the youth correctional facility. What people fail to realize is that institutionalized children are emotionally unstable and do not know how to function in a family. A boy from a Russian orphanage would know how to function in a Russian orphanage after living there for years. But he would not know how to function in an American family home, with completely new experiences and rules. Such a change would require teamwork from parent and child.

I also pointed out to my caseworker that such children are easily over stimulated and overwhelmed with abundance. Taking them to the grocery store for the first time would be an adventure. I would have to watch out for hyperactivity or exhaustion because of the stimulation of all the sights and sounds. In the orphanage, meals are a set amount without seconds. Most of the meals have very little, if any, meat, vegetables, and fruits. Fresh fruit and veggies would be available at all times in my house.

Another procedure in my home comes from my experience at the youth correctional facility. When my sons get home from school, they will have to be quiet in the bedroom for about fifteen minutes. They can read, take a nap, or listen to quiet, soft music. This is to get them to settle down after a stimulating day at school. Of course, this is flexible. Eventually, this procedure will end once they get adjusted to an American family lifestyle. People must remember that an institutionalized child is very different from a typical American child. Such children are emotionally unstable. My goal here is to get my sons to realize the need for quiet time rather than fear punishment.

For bedtime, I will tell them that nightmares or night terrors will be a good excuse for chocolate milk and cookies in the middle of the night. My message is that getting scared or crying in the middle of the night will be okay. We raid the refrigerator for a midnight snack; a change from bad thoughts to happy thoughts.

Their bedroom will have only the basic essentials such as a bed, nightstand, a dresser, and a desk. The walls will have only one or two pictures and maybe a Russian flag. There will be a few toys. The idea is to keep stimulation to a minimum and introduce them gradually to the concept of personal property, which does not exist in an orphanage.

The day after my adopted sons come home, we will start family therapy. My therapist, whom I have been working with for years, will be ready. What about the language problem in therapy? I already have this covered. First, such therapy with children is less verbal. There is play therapy and drawing pictures. Also remember, that emotional expression is just as important as verbal expression. I would also have an interpreter available.

The caseworker was impressed. She wrote a home study of acceptance for two brothers, ages seven to twelve, from Russia. Now all I had to do was find an international adoption agency that would work with me on such a placement.

My caseworker suggested I contact European Adoption Consultants (EAC). When I contacted the local EAC representative, she said EAC may not work with single men. Since she knew my caseworker from Parent Maker, she would review my home study and check with the director. About a week later, the EAC representative called me to tell me EAC does not work with single men as a general rule. She then spent the next fifteen minutes on the phone giving me advice, guidance, and pointers.

I was in shock! This was the first and only agency that rejected me yet tried to help me. I recommend EAC unconditionally to couples and single women. Although EAC would not work with me, I was treated with dignity and respect.

Before I contacted international adoption agencies for placements, I submitted my home study from Parent Maker to Immigration. When Immigration received my home study, they requested a copy of the Rimstone home study of denial and an assessment from a psychologist. Psychologist Dr. Anderson interviewed me, reviewed all my documents, and had several psychological instruments administered. He also reviewed the home studies from Rimstone and Parent Maker. His staff wrote up an evaluation using a template as if for court testimony. The psychologist specialized as an expert witness for courts. In May 2005 I received the final opinion from this licensed clinical/forensic psychologist.

> Mr. Garry White, a 54-year-old Anglo male seeking to be considered as a candidate to adopt a child or children, responded to all aspects of the evaluations in a direct and forthright manner. He provided a full and complete record of past evaluations and home studies. He completed all the information surveys, checklists and testing that was presented to him. He underwent clini-

cal evaluation as well. There was no significant indication from any of the data analyzed individually or the data reviewed collectively and comprehensively that he would not be an appropriate candidate for this adoptive program. Historically, he has been a foster parent and generally seemed to perform his parenting duties well. His anxiety reaction many years ago, without reoccurrence since that time should *not* play any credible or weighted value in his assessment as a candidate. He appears to be generally emotionally healthy and has clearly documented his strong and persistent desire to be a parent.

With that, Immigration approved me for an international adoption from Russia. With Immigration approval and an approved home study, I was ready, at least on paper. And with the psychological evaluation indicating that my anxiety attack years ago should not be considered, finding an international agency for a Russian placement should be easy, right?

Wrong! Almost all agencies worked only with single women, not single men. The standard excuse was that the country or region did not accept single men. I found that hard to believe, since from my research, I found a few single men who had adopted from Russia.

I contacted EAC again, since I had Immigration approval and a psychological assessment. The representative again said she would check with her director.

About a week later, the EAC director's secretary phoned me. She said her director wanted me to know why EAC will not work with single men. I was expecting the standard excuse: the country or region where the children come from does not accept single men. Instead, the secretary told me that EAC had placed with a single man a few years earlier, and it had been a disaster. EAC could not make a second such mistake, she said.

I could not believe my ears. This was the first international agency that had been honest and forthright with me. Although EAC rejected me twice, this agency tried to help me, and more importantly, was honest with me. Imagine how they treat those they do accept. I strongly recommend EAC. They have my highest respect and appreciation.

Following this episode, I found another international agency that worked with single men. When they found out about my mental history, they suddenly said Russia would not work with me.

Finally, after contacting another twenty agencies with Immigration approval, a positive psychological evaluation, and an approved home study, I found a religious international agency, Flowstone Agency, that would work with me in Russia. They provided me with single men references. I sent in $2,000 in fees, and the paperwork started. The agency then sent me its adoption packet for all the legal documents needed for Russia. The region of Russia where I would find my two sons was five hundred miles south of Moscow. Travel information was provided.

The bedroom was ready. I was making plans as to how I was going to tell all my friends and family that I was a new dad. I was on top of the world. I planned to tell only the very few who needed to know. Just before the placement, I would tell all my family and friends that I was going to be a dad.

Turned out, it was good I said nothing to family and friends. I received a letter from Immigration to stop all adoption processing and cancel any travel plans. I could not understand what happened. I e-mailed the American Embassy in Moscow to find out what had happened to my application. The reply was to contact the regional Immigration office that had processed my file. About a month later, I received a letter from Immigration. A staff member at the American Embassy in Moscow sent my file back with a recommendation to cancel my application. The reasons were centered on the Rimstone home study. Here are the reasons.

1. I admitted I would have difficulty managing a child who displayed psychotic features, persistent out-of-control behaviors or temper tantrums, and severe attention deficiency or hyperactivity.
2. My foster child, Mark, had to be returned to Child Protective Services due to out-of-control behaviors.
3. My psychiatric hospitalization in 1983.
4. A second psychiatric hospitalization in 1983.

5. My brother had been openly against the adoption plans due to my previous emotional breakdown.
6. Failed to discuss with my brother about care of a child in the event to my death.
7. My counselor (family therapist) diagnosed me as having a mild form of Asperger's Syndrome with poor social interaction skills.
8. The Rimstone home study indicated I appeared to be denying any and all possible complications and hardships with adopting a sibling group from a foreign country.

The embassy staff person noted that I had requested permission to adopt four children. The staff member did not condone the "shopping" for an approved home study to fulfill legal requirements. The Rimstone agency had disapproved me, so I went looking for another agency that would approve me. If an agency can make a mistake in approval, then an agency can make a mistake in disapproval. Almost all international agencies generally worked with single women only. Single men are not accepted regardless of the man's background.

The regional Immigration office decided to send my case to the Administrative Appeals Office (AAO). I was allowed to provide added information and request to appear before the AAO board to argue my case. I wrote a letter indicating the views of several licensed professionals and requested to appear before the board. After a few months, I asked my congressman to look into the matter since I had heard nothing. I was told my file had been lost. It seems my case number was mis-keyed into the computer systems. My congressman's staff member got the Immigration Administrative Appeals Office to put my case on the fast track. Finally, I got a decision. My request to appear before the board to argue my case was denied, and the recommendation of the embassy staff member was upheld.

This was the end. After trying for almost thirty years, it was all over. Luckily, during my therapy in 1984, the therapist had prepared me for such a disappointment. Also, my current therapist had prepared me by getting me to develop Plan B. It was time to put Plan B into operation.

Plan B was what I would do if rejected by Immigration. Without thinking, I changed the extra bedroom from a kid's bedroom to a guest bedroom. Next, I put away a bottle of champagne that I had been planning to use to celebrate becoming a dad. I tossed CDs that contained the song "The Impossible Dream." That music had been my theme for my quest to be a single dad. I put away all documents involving my failed quest.

Plan B: The Tucker Family

Once I did these things, I called my friends, the Tucker family, to tell them the bad news and to stay with them for a few nights. The major component of Plan B was the Tucker family. I could be a surrogate uncle to their three sons, Harvey, Al, and Wes. Plan B was now in full operation. For many years, this family has encouraged me in my efforts to be a single dad. They have permitted their three sons to be part of my life. I could do some things with them that allowed me to feel like a dad. This gave me satisfaction.

I first met the Tucker family when I was working on a master's degree. Joe Tucker was a work-study student in the computer lab, and I was majoring in computer science. I'll always remember the day he was pushing a computer cart down a hall of classrooms with his two little sons, Al and Harvey, ages four and five, riding the cart. The kids and their dad seemed to be having a good time together.

A few years later, Joe and his wife, Ann, had a third son, Wes. We all became close friends. When I was trying to adopt through CPS in 2001, Joe was one of my references. When I was making the transition from Child Protective Services to Rimstone Adoption Agency, Joe got me to go on a religious retreat. He was part of the retreat staff. During that retreat, we talked about my desire to be a dad through adoption. Everyone was very supportive and understanding. At that retreat, I told Joe I was going to try to adopt internationally, and Joe was supportive.

The Tucker family; from left to right: Joe, Ann, Harvey, Wes, Al; at McDonald Observatory in west Texas on their way with me to the Grand Canyon

Joe and Ann once allowed me to take their three sons, at the time ages fifteen, thirteen, and five, out for a day to shop at the malls. It was a lot of fun shopping and trying on things in the mall. Later, we ate Chinese, and I tried to teach the guys how to use chopsticks. We then went to a bookstore, where each of them selected a book to read. I noticed how parents frequently scan the store to see where their children are.

I was gratified that the kids stuck close by me, although Wes, the littlest, disappeared for a little while. Turned out he was behind a bookshelf and not far at all. It reminded me of Luke when I took him to the mall many years ago. The three boys were eager to show off their new books, shoes, and clothes to their parents.

Grand Canyon

As you can expect, I took the Tucker family to the Grand Canyon so Joe and his oldest son, Harvey, could hike across with me. It would be the six of us in a van. Riding with two teenagers and a four-year-old was an experience. All motels had to have a swimming pool. And Harvey had his learner's driving permit. He did some of the driving too.

There was a problem at the North Rim of the Grand Canyon. The lead driver for getting the cars to the South Rim had a panic attack. When Harvey heard this, he decided not to hike. He would drive his mother to the South Rim. I said, "No!" My response was automatic. I would drive his mother to the South Rim. Harvey was to hike with his dad, even if it meant I would miss out on the hike.

Weekend Substitute Parent

On another occasion, Joe asked me to stay with their three sons at their house while he and his wife were gone for the weekend. I fixed their sons' meals and made sure they got to bed on time. When I told them to get ready for bed, it turned out the guys wanted to stay up a little later to visit with me. I was flattered and proud that I meant that much to them. They all went off to bed after I told them I would not sing them a lullaby song off key and not tell them a scary bedtime story. Then I tucked them in and went off to sleep on the couch. People who are not parents don't know how pleasant such a day as this can be.

Harvey

During the summer of 2005, I helped teach their oldest son, Harvey, how to drive a car. One time, when he was getting upset while driving, I taught him that he should pull over in a safe area and park until he felt in control again. On another occasion, Harvey took both hands off the steering wheel to express himself. When he stopped the car and got out, I told him how dangerous that had been. Through all the scary moments, we always arrived at our destinations in one piece, and tranquilizers were not needed. I look forward to teaching their next son, Al, how to drive.

*Harvey Tucker, reader to hike
across the Grand Canyon*

Harvey made a grade of *D* in chemistry. I suggested he stay with me for four days so I could tutor him since I had once been a high school chemistry teacher. I learned that he understood the concepts. His problem was the math. He would divide when he should multiply and vice versa. If there was one thing Harvey taught me during those four days, it was that my lifestyle would dramatically change as a single dad. Instead of doing the dishes once a week, we did it every day. Instead of taking out the trash twice a month, it was once, almost twice, a week.

One evening at the Tucker family house, Harvey and I were sitting outside on a bench. Harvey had problems at work he wanted to tell me about. I listened. He was in deep distress and upset. When he finished, I told him an old Egyptian proverb. When you have a problem, sleep on it. Many times when you sleep on a problem, insight and solutions can come to you, something about your subconscious working on the problem. When you wake up, you may have the insight to the problem. What actions are needed become clear. He needed to relax and go to bed and get a good night's sleep. He did.

Harvey is the type of friend I would want my sons to have. At the age of sixteen, he started an after-school job. After two years, he bought a car and is in college, still working the same job and paying for most of his education and needs. Harvey is great with all his younger brothers and cousins. Once, when I took the Tucker family out to eat, Harvey wanted to take his younger brothers out to a movie and buy them snacks at the theater, out of his own hard-earned money. You can see why I would want my sons, if I ever have any, to have Harvey as a friend.

Al

Al is also in the Boy Scouts. With my help, he was able to decide on an Eagle project. We would laugh about how soon he would have his Eagle Court of

Honor, a big party. I suggested he have a display with pictures of his scouting experience, a slideshow, and scouting centerpieces on the tables. He did make Eagle.

On a Scout campout, Al had difficulty hiking. When we came to a stream, he feared he would slip and fall. I handed him my hiking stick, which I always used at the Grand Canyon, put my hands under his armpits, and gently pushed him on. I told him to think of my hiking stick as a portable handrail. As we walked slowly, I told him how, at the Grand Canyon, I always hike very slowly to enjoy the scenery.

On another Scout outing, the Troop was to explore a wild cave with experienced cavers, like myself. The cave was a maze that kids could safely enjoy. Al did not want to go. I knew he was scared that this adventure might be beyond his physical and mental limits. I knew better. I'd explored this cave several times with youth before. I urged him to go, and when he had enough, I would bring him out. He finally agreed. We entered the cave, and he did fine until he encountered a tight hole that he had to crawl through. As we approached the entrance, where we saw daylight, I urged him to try some crawl holes off to the side. At first he refused, but I urged him to go as far as he could, then just come back. He did and learned a valuable lesson about knowing one's limits. The caving trip was a success.

Al coming out of a cave where he learned he could do more than he thought

Like his older brother, Al has a work ethic. He kept talking about getting a job so he could buy a car and pay for his education like his older brother. On one outing to the mall, Al hit several stores, picking up employment applications, with no urging from me. I enjoyed coaching him on job interviews. Having been an interviewer myself, I told him what employers were looking for: someone reliable and honest. If the interviewers asked him why he had not gotten a job sooner? I suggested he tell the truth: he was working on his Boy Scout Eagle project.

Wes

The youngest son, Wes, now age seven, and I have a tradition. I always pick him up and hold him above my head. I ask if he is bigger than me.

He will say, "Yes."

I then hold him at eye level and say, "I'm not sure. Are you sure you are bigger than me?"

I then hold him above my head, and he will say, "Yes."

One evening, I forgot to do this. He came up to me and lifted his arms and reminded me to pick him up. He felt safe with me holding him up high above my head. When I put him down, I told him that one day he would break my back since he would be too heavy. Every time I do this, I get a joy out of seeing a smile on his face.

Wes – Are you bigger than me?

Christmas

As my therapist put it, I put my money where my mouth is. When I committed to the Tucker sons as an alternative to being a dad, I meant it. At Christmas, I gave Harvey, Al, and Wes envelopes. On each was written, "Big things come in small packages." Inside was another envelope. On it was written, "What can never be destroyed, lost, or stolen?" Inside that envelope was another envelope. On it was written, "An education, a good investment." Inside these last envelopes were checks to go toward their education. They were really surprised.

Al's comment was, "This cannot be real."

These three sons are worth an investment in their education.

A Problem or a Gift?

A problem I discovered with Harvey and Al, ages seventeen and nineteen, was that my brain told me they were very mature and responsible young adults. But my heart told me they were still the two little boys, ages four and six, I had first seen on the computer cart moving down a hall of classrooms. If one of them ended up in a wheelchair for life, I saw myself taking care of him for life. I understand why an American soldier adopted an Iraqi orphan with cerebral palsy and how parents are able to care for their adult handicapped children.

A close friend, Johnny May, has a very severely handicapped son, age fifteen. Johnny always takes his son places in a wheelchair, bathes, feeds, and changes him. Once you see a child as yours, any problems he or she has will be accepted.

Johnny May has known for years of my desire to adopt. When he heard I was having problems with CPS, he offered to travel and let the caseworkers know that I would welcome a handicapped child.

Supporting My Quest

Joe and Ann's three sons have long known of my desire to be a dad. Five years ago, Al, at the age of twelve, told me I would make a great dad. The fact that he had known me for so long, often in the role of surrogate dad, made those words all the more gratifying. But it also hurt because Al's opinion meant nothing to Rimstone and Immigration. Over the years, the two older sons would ask me how the adoption was going.

My response was always, "Things are moving forward with a lot of ups and downs, like a roller coaster." Better to say nothing and have a surprise than to say something and have a disappointment.

Joe and Ann introduced me to a single adoptive mother from church who had never married. She had adopted a mixed-race child. She agreed that being single by divorce was more acceptable in our society than never having been married. She pointed out the old-maid image of single women who never marry. When I told her all my reasons for wanting to be a father, she said that I was the first person in her life who truly understood why she had wanted to be a parent.

There is more to parenting than just doing fun and interesting things, like hiking across the Grand Canyon. On the TV show *Fantasy Island,* there was an episode about an orphanage director's fantasy to find a home for her last two orphans. While the two orphans did fun and interesting things with families, the director washed their clothes and had dinner ready for them when they got back. In the evening, after the adventures with families, the director listened to what they had done and made sure they did their schoolwork and chores. In the end, the kids wanted to live with the director, a single woman, instead of the families. There is a difference between playing with the kids and being a parent to them.

Eventually, I realized that Plan B really was not working. Al phoned me that his Scout troop had elected him into the fraternal Order of the Arrow (OA). He was excited and wanted me to know since I was already a member. He wanted me to take him to his Ordeal. This was great. I would have him all weekend for his Ordeal campout and be the one to place the OA shawl on him. It would almost be like a dad-and-son adventure.

A few weeks later, Joe called to tell me how excited he was. The adults in the troop had elected him to OA. He too would be at the Ordeal with son Al. I then realized that I was just a very close friend, or more like an uncle. I would not be having a dad-and-son experience on that OA campout. I had to try again to adopt internationally.

A week later, parked in a restaurant parking lot, I wept and bared my soul to Joe about my desire to adopt and the hurdles that had been placed in my way. Joe learned of my hospitalization and all the hardships I had gone through for almost thirty years. I told him how I had signed myself into a psychiatric hospital because it was in the best interest of Jerry. Unfortunately, people saw that as an unforgivable sin.

Joe learned about Mt. San Francisco, eighty miles south of the Grand Canyon, where I'd had to make a decision about my foster son, Mark. I told him how my foster son had been used against me, even though two two-parent families had not been able to deal with him either. Mark had required residential treatment. People ignored the fact that my reason had been to act in his best interest. I had been in no hurry for him to leave.

My brain was wired to be a dad, and I could not change that. I had to try again. When I told Joe I had no one to sign a document indicating responsibility of my sons in the event of my death, Joe immediately said he and his wife would be very happy to sign such a document. He also wanted to know my caseworker's phone number. When I asked why, he said he wanted to find out exactly what he needed to write so it would work this time. After talking with Joe, I began the process of another home study, psychological assessment, and references.

My Big Final Try: International Again

I first checked with my congressman's constituent liaison. He told me that the immigration officer suggested I reapply with new information. A second home study from a different caseworker and a second psychological assessment would be my new information. Surely, all issues would be resolved.

I contacted an old college fraternity brother who was a retired immigration judge. He said that reapplying with new information was a good idea. It would be a different adjudication. I am not a lawyer and do not know what he meant by *adjudication*. But it sounded good.

I was uneasy about telling my family therapist. Would he see me as just trying hopelessly, or would he be supportive? Turns out he was supportive. He knew I could not quit. A point in therapy I kept making was that he too would never give up on his children. What true, good parent would?

We discussed another psychological assessment from a second licensed clinical/forensic psychologist. I suggested one, Dr. Rogers, after researching local psychologists. He agreed. Later, I found out that he knew the psychologist.

The assessment methods were:

- Clinical interview
- Minnesota Multiphasic Personality Inventory-2 (MMPI-II)
- Millon Clinical Multiaxial Inventory-3 (MCMI-III)
- Beck Depression Inventory (BDI)
- Review of records
- Consultation with my family therapist

Some of Dr. Roger's conclusions were:

There is nothing in Mr. White's psychological history that should be of concern in evaluating him as a potential adoptive parent. [He did discuss my brief psychiatric hospitalization in 1983 in his assessment report.]

His MMPI-II profile indicates that Garry is a sociable person who likes to project a positive attitude about life. In addition, his response pattern is also characteristic of people who tend to not be interested in the expression or discussion of feelings.

It appears that Garry prefers to be seen by others as composed, virtuous, and conventional in his behavior. Individuals with profiles similar to Garry's tend toward being uncomfortable in showing a lot of emotion. While Garry has deep feelings inside, he has tended to rely on a lighthearted interpersonal style that avoids the expression of deep feelings. While his profile matches those of people who are most comfortable with their analytical or intellectual sides, Garry noted that he has been working in his counseling to learn to be more expressive of feelings and empathy.

The MCMI-III profile matched the MMPI-II result in not finding evidence of any psychological conflicts and there was no support for a clinical diagnosis.

This evaluation provides support for the conclusion that Mr. White is emotionally healthy and is not currently experiencing any psychiatric condition. The data from this assessment—when combined with the data from previous psychological assessments and home studies—demonstrates that across time Mr. White has consistently been shown to be psychologically fit to be a potential adoptive parent. This individual's social and emotional stability, combined with his long-held motivation to be a parent, suggest that Garry White is an appropriate candidate for becoming an adoptive parent.

References

By now the reader should realize that every time I tried to adopt, I had to get references. Thank God, I have friends who believe in me and will, over and over again, write reference letters for me. By 2001, all my lifelong friends knew of my attempts over the past twenty-five-plus years to adopt and the circumstances surrounding my 1983 mental illness. At least once during those years, I asked them to be references.

A method I used to decide on references for this go-around was to remind them that I was getting a PhD and had a job that provided me with plenty of time to be a single dad. "What are your thoughts about me adopting now?" I asked them. Instead of listening to *what* they said, I listened to *how* they said it. People will always be polite. But the truth is in how they say it.

Unfortunately, I had to cut people out as references. There were at least two families who, if they read this book, will realize they were cut out. I know they will be hurt. But I needed references who were absolutely supportive.

This time I had to get four references. The first was Joe Tucker, who had been my steady reference for so many of these attempts to adopt. Here are some of the things he wrote in his most current reference.

> During the summertime, we spend a lot of time at Garry's house. Garry lives right next to the river, and he is always inviting friends

to come and tube the river. He hosted my oldest son at his house last summer to tutor him and help him finish a chemistry course he was taking during the summer. He also had Harvey over to show him the campus of the university where he works. Harvey came home and said that he got a lot out of his visit and said that Garry was very supportive of him in his college goals.

I have seen Garry meld well with other adults in my family, my brothers, and my sisters. He has joined over the last five years in a number of our family outings and seems to get along with everyone—kids included. My boys look up to Garry as a friend and a companion.

Garry is a very caring and compassionate person. Garry is someone who always puts someone else's interests before his. He understands the dynamics of what it takes to care for and love someone else before himself.

Garry has never during the time that we have known him displayed any mental or physiological abnormality. Garry has told us that many years ago he checked into a hospital for mental illness. We would have never have known unless he told us.

The second reference is the personal editor for this book. He has known of my desire to adopt for almost ten years. With that knowledge, he supported the idea of writing this book. He and his wife have written several references.

The third reference was a retired coworker. He too has known of my desire to adopt for almost ten years. This reference has given me great insight into being an adoptive parent. He and his wife adopted a seven-year-old boy from Child Protective Services. Today, their son is a successful educator. This was the third time I asked him to be a reference.

My fourth reference was my family therapist. He has written at least four reference letters, more than any of the others.

Another Home Study

I was uneasy when I contacted my caseworker at Parent Maker. Would she see me as desperate, or would she be supportive? I told her she needed a new home study, and to my surprise, she agreed. She had another caseworker in mind to do a home study. Later, I learned that this second caseworker was hesitant to take my case after reviewing a copy of my file and report from Immigration. But after she got to know me, she wrote a very positive home study that quoted my 1983 attending psychiatrist, my family therapist, and two licensed clinical/forensic psychologists.

In this last home study with Parent Maker, five concerns from the Rimstone International home study were listed. Here they are.

1. Uncertainty that other countries would accept a single male applicant with a history of mental health issues.
2. Lack of a trial period with international adoptions in which the child and prospective parent can be closely monitored before legal finalization.
3. Doubts by the worker that Garry understood how adoption could impact him emotionally, mentally, and physically.
4. Doubts by the worker that Garry understood how institutionalization would impact children's ability to regulate their emotions and behaviors.
5. Belief by worker that Garry had awkward social interaction skills.

We'll get back to these concerns later, along with the issue of my 1983 mental illness.

Here are highlights of my last home study:

Garry will assume full responsibility for the medical and financial needs of his children after placement. He is knowledgeable of the laws of the State of Texas pertaining to international adoption, the requirements of the Bureau of Citizenship and Immigrant Services, and the adoption process in general.

Garry has received pre-adoptive counseling on the risks associated with adopting internationally, including expenses, difficulties and delays, and an unknown history of the children. Garry is also aware of the post-placement requirements and plans to have regular contact with his social worker once children are placed in his home. These contacts, including visits in the home, will cover counseling and education related to helping his children adjust into the home, family, and culture.

His references all highly recommended him as an adoptive parent.

Immigration

Now that I had a new second home study by another caseworker, a new second positive psychological assessment, more great references, and a different adjudication (whatever that means), I was very optimistic. Who would reject the conclusions and recommendations of two forensic psychologists, the 1983 attending psychiatrist, and a licensed family therapist? These four mental health practitioners all indicated that my 1983 illness should carry no weight in evaluating my ability to be an adoptive parent and that I was emotionally and psychologically fit to be an adoptive parent. I sent my application with the $670 fee.

Four months later, I still had not heard from Immigration. I contacted my congressman to find out what was going on. Immigration said a letter had been sent to me requesting copies of references and a copy of the previous denied home study. I never got that letter. I requested clarification on which previous home study was requested, Rimstone or the previous Parent Maker. I never got a reply on that clarification, but they did say they had my correct address.

I had my caseworker send in copies of my references and a notarized copy of my previous Parent Maker home study that had been denied by Immigration. Again, I did not hear from Immigration. From my congressman, I learned that Immigration was claiming it never received the previous denied home study.

I called Immigration and told them I would meet an officer in the lobby of their building in San Antonio, Texas, to personally hand them the previous denied home study and a printed copy of my address. Turns out they did have a wrong address for me. The officer said the Rimstone home study was what they wanted, so I gave them a copy. A few months later, I received notice of Immigration's decision.

Now What? The Big Debate

Decision for Second Application

Upon consideration, it is ordered that your Application for Advance Processing of Orphan Petition (Form I-600A) be DENIED for the following reasons: See Attachment.

You may, if you wish, appeal this decision on a Form I-290B. You must submit such an appeal to THIS OFFICE with a filing fee of $385.00. If you do not file within the time allowed, this decision is final. Appeal in your case may be made to the Office of Administrative Appeals (AAO) in Washington, D.C. It must reach this office within 30 calendar days from the date this notice is served.

My previous Parent Maker home study, which had been denied earlier by Immigration, was evaluated for this application. My current Parent Maker home study was ignored. The officer quoted the notarization date on the last page instead of the completion date on the front page of the home study. Remember, I had my caseworker send in the previous Parent Maker home study thinking that it was the one they wanted when they really wanted a copy of the Rimstone International home study.

Most of the reasons were the reasons for the first Immigration denial. The opinions of one Rimstone international social worker were the basis for the decision of denial. Immigration ignored the references they requested, the second approved home study by a second caseworker, and four licensed mental health practitioners.

I am a fighter when it comes to my desire to be a dad. The question was how I was going to appeal and with what facts to argue for overturning the decision.

Second Appeal

My caseworker suggested I see a lawyer. I did have a lifelong friend, Scoutmaster Frank Fox, who was a lawyer and knew of my desire to adopt. He pointed out that my background in scouting was completely ignored when this decision had been reached. He told me to do several things:

1. Write up my Scout resume.

2. Write up my responses to the five Rimstone concerns.

3. Get my caseworker to address those five Rimstone concerns in more detail.

4. Explain my position as to the number of children I desired.

5. Get a letter from my brother as to his position on my desire to adopt.

He would then write a legal brief for my appeal.

The Five Rimstone Concerns

Here are the five Rimstone concerns my caseworker noted from the Rimstone International home study that denied my approval.

1. *Uncertainty that other countries would accept a single male applicant with a history of mental health issues.*

   Caseworker's response:

   According to Mr. White, Flowstone Adoption Agency accepted Mr. White's 2004 Parent Maker Home Study. He informs me that Flowstone Adoption Agency indicated that a placement from Russia was possible. He further informs me that he applied to Russia with U.S. Immigration, and his understanding is that Flowstone Adoption Agency is waiting for approval from his appeal to Immigration.

Mr. White advises that, prior to the Rimstone home study, another agency, Limestone Adoption Services, believed a placement was possible with the Ukraine. He informs me that they had a copy of his Rimstone home study that disclosed his history of mental health issues, and that Limestone Adoption Services told him to have his Rimstone home study rewritten for an international placement.

My Response:

Rimstone already knew my mental history and other issues from my Rimstone domestic foster/adopt home study. I can only conclude that Rimstone felt that a country would accept a single, male applicant with a history of mental health issues. Why else would Rimstone proceed with an international home study knowing these facts?

2. *Lack of "trial period" with international adoptions in which the child and prospective parent can be closely monitored before legal finalization.*

Caseworker's response:

After placement, there is a three-year monitoring period by a social worker to help address and resolve any difficulties in the placement.

Mr. White points out that, because of his mental history, he understands, recognizes, and knows what to do when it comes to his mental problems. He further knows of community support mechanisms. He states that counseling and therapy will be available as needed.

My response:

The fear here is that problems will arise after placement. This is highly unlikely due to my caseworker's response above, my master's degree in psychology, my work with troubled youth at a youth correctional facility, my fostering of a disturbed child longer than two two-parent families, my work with a therapist, and my graduate courses in special education, adolescent psychology, and educational psychology.

The Rimstone caseworker forgot to mention that there is a four- to five-week period in the foreign country to evaluate if there is a good match.

3. *Doubts by the worker that Mr. White understood how adoption could impact him emotionally, mentally, and physically.*

Caseworker's response:

I believe that Mr. White does sufficiently understand the impact of an adoption. For a year and a half, he was a foster parent to a child with serious mental problems that at one time required residential treatment. I believe that experience has given him the insight necessary to understand that adoption is a life-changing event.

My response:

This contradicts the Rimstone domestic home study for foster/adopt. That home study states: "Mr. White is kind and calm, he fully understands what types of behaviors may arise with a child, but he is ready to nurture a child and help him grow up to be a healthy man ... I, (domestic caseworker), believe he (Garry White) has a relatively firm understanding of what he may face when a child is placed with him because of his previous fostering experience. He did not provide quick responses to the questions asked but instead pondered them. He understands that there may be situations that may arise with behaviors, and if he is unable to deal with them, he will seek guidance, support, and suggestions from the agency, the child's therapist, and his family and friends. He is willing to attend additional training opportunities to educate himself concerning medical conditions specific to the child."

Along with my current caseworker, there is a second caseworker who also believes I sufficiently understand the impact of an adoption.

4. *Doubts by the worker that Garry understood how institutionalization would impact children's ability to regulate their emotions and behaviors.*

Caseworker's response:

Garry advises that he has educated himself on such topics since 2004. I have discussed these issues with him, and my impression is that he is very knowledgeable in this area.

My response:

An impact of institutionalization on children is institutional autism and delayed sensory development. Such children are generally developmentally delayed and crave attention. These children are easily over-stimulated and overwhelmed by abundance. You have to be careful in taking them to the supermarket. The characteristics of these disorders are well within my abilities and limits. In fact, I look forward to having such sons.

Older adoptive children tend to exhibit age-inappropriate behavior. For example, a twelve-year-old may want to ride on my back as if he were six. Another example, he may pretend to be helpless with simple things like tying a shoelace. This is a very good sign. What my son is doing is making up for lost time with me. He is regressing back to age six to live that part of his life again with me. For my back's sake, I just hope the twelve-year-old is not too heavy.

Every day I will spend time teaching my sons English, the same way I was taught for my dyslexia. These methods are multi-sensory that stimulate the brain. Here are the methods.

1. Put blocks of letters in hands and let them feel and play with the letter blocks.
2. Trace the letters in sand or on sandpaper.
3. Write letters with colored crayons and say sound.
4. I trace a letter on his back with my finger, and he writes it in the air and says the sound. For example, I will trace the letter *C* on his back. He traces it in the air and says the sound. I then do the letter *A,* then *T.* I will repeat these letters faster and faster until he fully says the word *cat.*
5. Shake his right hand and say, "Right." Then shake his left and say, "Left" over and over again. This will develop a sense of dexterity. This can help problems with reversals. I will have to set the example and do it too at first.

These multi-sensory methods will help provide sensory-motor and speech stimulation. Learning phonics this way will also address institutional autism, development delay, language development, cognitive issues, sensory integration disorder (SID), and more importantly, attachment to me. Most institutionalized children suffer from many of these problems, especially attachment disorders.

5. *Belief by worker that Garry had awkward social interaction skills.*

Caseworker's response:

I do not characterize Mr. White's social interaction skills as "awkward." In fact, I found Mr. White to be engaging, welcoming, polite, and friendly. He does have Asperger's disorder; however, it is mild, and the therapist who made the diagnosis has indicated that the disorder would not prevent him from being a successful single parent of an adopted child. Moreover, the same therapist has been counseling Mr. White for over four years around his stress management and his desire to be a parent. That therapist has written a letter recommending that Mr. White be considered as an adoptive parent. In his letter, he stated that Mr. White is warm, and he has good knowledge of what children need emotionally.

My Response:

Awkward social interaction skills? What do my current references, references from my

Rimstone domestic home study, two Parent Maker caseworkers, a family therapist (who has worked with me for years and diagnosed me as having mild Asperger's Syndrome), and two psychologists say? Joe Tucker indicated to the contrary in his reference letter.

To lead five groups of ten-plus people on a two-week trip to the Grand Canyon requires good social interaction skills.

In contrast to the Rimstone international home study, the Rimstone domestic home study states: "He appears to be able to make friends, though it may be a small group of individuals and maintains lasting friendships, and is reportedly close to his brother and mother."

From a professional perspective, I have good people skills. Over the past five years I have co-authored research papers with six other faculty members. Junior faculty members are always coming to me for assistance with their research.

Why Two or Three Children?

My dream was for a sibling group. Three is the ideal maximum I might possibly handle. Considering the stress that international adoptive children experience, such a sibling group can provide a good support group for one another, especially upon my death.

Although my sons need siblings they can relate to and have after my death, I understand that three can be a real handful. My friend Joe Tucker has three sons. Having spent a two-week Grand Canyon vacation in a van with his family, I realize that three sons may be too many to have all at once. My current home study is for two brothers. This is a more realistic number, given my age. My hopes were to have a third later if all goes well.

My Brother's Position

When my lawyer told me to get a letter from my brother stating his position on my desire to adopt, I became concerned. My brother had seen me in the psychiatric hospital years ago. Over the years, he was always worried that it might happen again if I adopt. At first, after my hospitalization, he was against adoption. Over the years, he developed an attitude of *proceed with caution*. He and his wife were always politely supportive with limitations. They questioned whether I could handle a severely disturbed child or more than one. At the same time, they frequently busied themselves trying to fix me up with their women friends.

I stressed to Frank, my lawyer, that whatever my brother wrote, positive or negative, I was not to know. This would put reliability and validity to whatever he said and would avoid family conflict. I contacted my brother and told him of the developments with my international adoption and said I needed to discuss this with him.

When the day for this discussion with Larry arrived, I was concerned about what his position on adoption might be, given all these years since my anxiety attack. As we began our discussion, my brother indicated that he believed that I would make a great dad to one or two boys.

My brother said I was socially awkward yet very sociable. I had more lifelong friends than he or anyone else he knew. It sounded like the issue was resolved.

Next we discussed the fears of a failed placement. He was concerned that I might get a child with problems beyond what I could deal with. I pointed out that, statistically, around 15 percent of placements with older children fail. And with my background with troubled youth, my educational background, and my plans to get into family therapy before problems started, the odds would be much less. He agreed and told me his fears were lessened, if not completely set aside.

Another fear we had to resolve was my hospitalization. During the past twenty-four years, there had been two incidents during which he feared I would need to be hospitalized. Larry tended to overreact when I got excited and needed to get a good night's sleep. Neither incident involved dysfunctional behavior. One was the news of getting a great job. The second was getting upset with my niece. I wanted to have some quality time with her, and she was only interested in herself. I did take sleep medication during those two events. My brother saw the next morning that all was well. My point is that those two incidents proved that I know when I need a good night's sleep and will act accordingly.

He pointed out that I was dependent on medication to avoid mental problems and be able to function. I responded that he needed blood pressure medicine to stay alive. He agreed; issue resolved.

Fox's Appeal Brief

Here is a summary of my lawyer's appeal brief.

1. Dr. White is a highly educated, well-meaning adult male who has the best interests of his future adoptive child/children as his utmost goal.

2. Dr. White fully understands the uncertainties of foreign adoption and is willing to work to all ends to make this adoption a success.

3. Dr. White has met with an adoptive family (from a Boy Scout Troop) of an eleven-year-old Russian boy and his thirteen-year-old sister. Dr. White has also corresponded with other adoptive parents of Russian/Ukrainian children. Doug Smith of Abilene, Texas, is a single, male adoptive parent, who advises Dr. White to "go for it."

4. Dr. White has cared for himself for fifty-seven years and is aware of his strengths and weaknesses and has undertaken remedial action to overcome the weaknesses (mental

issues) that Rimstone identified. Dr. White has maintained a professional relationship with his therapist, who supported him and believes Dr. White is ready to become an adoptive parent. On June 26, 2006, Dr. Rogers, PhD, conducted a psychological evaluation of Dr. White, and he concludes that Dr. White is "emotionally healthy" and "psychologically fit to be a potential adoptive parent." Dr. Rogers concludes, "Garry White is an appropriate candidate for becoming an adoptive parent."

5. Dr. White's extensive experience with at-risk youth places him in a better position than most two-parent adoptive families.

6. Dr. White is open and willing to accept professional assistance in making the adoption process work.

7. Parent Maker has reviewed the report by Rimstone and wrote a reply on August 31, 2006, which includes up-to-date home visits and up-to-date professional evaluations recommending him for adoptive placement.

8. Dr. White has considered the possibility of his early demise and has secured the contingency plan of an alternative placement in the community for his family. The reservations of Rimstone are those of archaic preconceptions that should not be perpetuated in the year 2007. Dr. White is a kind, gentle, caring man

who would go to end of the earth to make his adoptive family, whether it be one, two, or three children, a successful undertaking.

With the legal brief and other documents, my appeal was sent in on time. After seven months of waiting, I finally received the official decision from the Immigration Administrative Appeals Office. As you can imagine, waiting and not knowing when a decision would be made, even after getting my congressman and senator to find out, was hell.

Plan B Again

Upon careful review of all evidence contained in the record, the Office of Administrative Appeals (AAO) finds that serious concerns exist relating to the applicant's ability to provide proper care to an orphan. The AAO finds that the evidence presented by the applicant fails to overcome those concerns. Accordingly, the AAO finds that the applicant has failed to establish that he would provide proper parental care to an adopted orphan as set forth in section 101(b) (1)(F)(i) of the Act and 8 C.F.R 204.3(a)(2).

In visa petition proceedings, the burden of proof rests solely with the applicant. See section 291 of the Act, 8 U.S.C. 1361. The applicant has failed to meet his burden of proof in the present matter. The appeal will therefore be dismissed and the application will be denied.

ORDER: The appeal will be dismissed. The application will be denied.

Issues were:

1. My mental illness of twenty-four years ago.
2. Unable to consider the fact that I might find myself being overwhelmed with the multiple responsibilities and needs of three children.
3. Awkward social interaction skills.
4. Asperger's Syndrome, which includes concrete intellectual processing with poor social interaction skills.
5. Unclear whether my coping strategies would be effective when parenting one, two, or three children with histories of neglect and possible abuse that could lead to challenging behaviors such as emotional reactivity, out-of-control behavior, and hyperactivity or attention-deficit characteristics.
6. Lack of the two psychological assessments providing details or information relating to the applicant's previous treatment and hospitalizations or their causes.

The AAO finds that the evidence in the record presents serious concerns regarding the applicant's ability to provide care to an orphan. The concerns raised in the Rimstone home study report relating to the applicant's ability to provide proper parental care to an orphan child are documented, well reasoned, valid, and material.

My Rebuttal

The reason the two psychological assessments lack details or information relating to my previous treatment and hospitalizations or causes is that the two licensed psychologists saw it as a nonissue. This was pointed out in the reports. My therapist, whom I have worked with for years, also agrees it is a non-issue. What qualifies the Rimstone caseworker and Immigration to say my 1983 hospitalization is an issue?

The AAO decision brief was solely based on the impressions and opinions of one Rimstone international caseworker. The AAO totally disregarded the opinions, conclusions, and recommendations from four licensed mental health practitioners. Obviously, Immigration gave more weight to one caseworker then the combined weight of:

1. Attending psychiatrist, Dr. Joug
2. Attending family therapist
3. Clinical/forensic psychologist requested by Immigration, Dr. Anderson
4. Second clinical/forensic psychologist, Dr. Rogers

5. Psychological assessment requested by Immigration
6. Second psychological assessment that is consistent with the first
7. Approved international home study by a licensed master's level social worker
8. Second approved international home study by another licensed master's level social worker
9. References Immigration requested
10. Rimstone-approved domestic home study

There appears to be stereotyping, prejudice, and bias. How else can you explain ignoring all these solid references?

My lawyer, Frank, told me to get written comments from my therapist and psychologist about the decision. He would then send the comments to Immigration.

Here is what my family therapist stated in his letter to Immigration.

> First, let me say that the agency (US CIS), and one home study cited in the appeals letter has inappropriately used my initial diagnosis of my patient in regards to the label Asperger's disorder. The agency used a sentence from the Rimstone home study and used part of a sentence, "the patient has been diagnosed with Asperger's disorder..." and ran with it as a backdrop to the appeals denial. My sense

of what happened later is that the agency used this term and the home studier's definition of it in deciding the patient's viability as an adoptive parent. This is inappropriate. In my letter Asperger's was diagnosed as "mild" and while the patient meets the criteria, several clinicians stated this would not affect his ability to warmly parent. Given the wide spectrum of this particular disorder, with some sophistication, and given the absence of bias, the agency might have attempted to learn what the term actually meant. The home studier did no psychometric testing, had brief interviews with the patient, and was not a licensed psychologist to make such a pronouncement in recommending against the patient. Certainly the agency, given the important role it plays, should have leaned toward the recommendations of the licensed clinical psychologists over the home studier. This seems unfair and without expertise.

Secondly, four clinicians (I, two licensed clinical psychologists, as well as the physician who treated him over twenty years ago) stated the patient presents with no mental illness. He was treated briefly twenty-four years ago, but with no recurring episodes and given the high level of his emotional functioning, this episode also proved to run in the background of the agency's rationale for his denial. This, again, is suggestive of a lack of expertise.

How are you supposed to know what to do? In which way are you qualified to make these life-affecting decisions? An appropriate model is to listen to the clinicians and the variety of responses, not to camp on the side of one home studier, which is very suggestive of bias. Is it the fact that he is a male? Single men make terrific parents. Is there a bias against a single mental status episode decades ago, which in turn labels a good and caring person as mentally ill? If that is the case, the agency is living in the dark ages. This person's episode was transient and well managed by the patient.

Although the appeal has denied permission to the patient to adopt internationally, I am hoping that you will ask all field personnel in your office, top to bottom, to look carefully at your biases and the policies they create.

Here is what the psychologist, Dr. Rogers, stated in his letter to me.

> In my reading of the appeal decision, it appears that great weight was given to the Rimstone home study report. Apparently, in that report the home study preparer expressed reservations about your preparedness to be an adoptive parent. The concerns seemed to be centered on several issues: the possible significance of your psychiatric hospitalization in 1983, your possessing "awkward social interaction skills," and your ability to manage stress.

First, after reviewing again the results of my psychological testing with you, I stand by my conclusion that you were—at the time of assessment—psychologically healthy and were emotionally fit to become an adoptive parent. Further, since the results of my assessment of you matched those of Dr. Anderson's previous assessment, I have every reason to believe that this conclusion is both valid and likely to be an enduring result.

Second, even the Rimstone home study preparer noted that you had "made tremendous gains" in the last twenty years. It is my belief that your dedication to psychotherapy and personal growth should make the issue of a hospitalization in 1983 a nonfactor. Your therapist documented that you have successfully acquired skills for coping with stress and anxiety.

Third, it appears to me that too much has been made of you having a mild form of Asperger's Syndrome. Your social skills are not poor, in my opinion. Further, many people with mild forms of Asperger's are quite successful parents. My assessment of you supported the likelihood that you could be a warm and engaged parent.

Garry, whatever you decide to do from here regarding your dream of becoming an adoptive parent, I hope that you won't interpret this negative outcome as reflecting negatively on who you are as a person. Your ongoing therapy and several psychological evaluations have provided you with positive validation of your many positive qualities.

My lawyer saw little hope. He saw no grounds to appeal. After thirty years of trying, it was all over.

Implementing Plan B Again

Like the first time I implemented Plan B, I moved things out of sight in my home. I again threw away the CDs with my theme songs of "Impossible Dream" and "I Will Follow Him." I planned a "ceremony of loss" to bring closure to thirty years of trying to be a single dad. Next, I e-mailed my brother, my caseworker at Parent Maker, and two close friends (one being my personal editor for this book) telling them the bad news and plans for the ceremony of loss.

I phoned the Tucker family. It just so happened they were leaving on a camping trip the next day. Joe insisted that I come along. We got to the campsite on a ranch. It was a nice day, and we did the usual camping activities. That evening, after dinner, we played a game of dominos. I won.

After lunch the next day, I decided to take a walk. I came upon a hunting blind with a chair inside. I sat in the chair and looked out over the meadow, where I saw a couple of cows grazing. Then I did the unthinkable: I cursed God. "Damn you!" I cried. "Why did you abandon me? All I wanted was to be a dad to a few homeless boys."

I swore then that I would set the record straight by writing this book and that I would never give up fighting the system. My thoughts then turned to the Tucker family and how important they were to me. I could still enjoy activities with their three sons. I could still tuck Wes into bed every evening, joke with him about not singing a lullaby off-key, and pick him up over my head.

About an hour later, Joe came by with his truck to see how I was doing. He brought me lunch and said to come on back to camp when I was ready. When I got back to camp, we had dinner and another game of dominos. I won.

About a week later, Joe had me take his middle son, Al, to his Eagle Board of Review. Joe was giving me quality time with his son. I was there when the board approved Al's completed Eagle project and signed his Eagle Rank papers. He was now an Eagle Scout, pending paperwork from National.

Myself and Al Tucker in front of his Eagle display

My therapist suggested I take an anti-depression medication because I was starting to show serious signs of depression. I decided I wouldn't because to do so would validate AAO's decision. Instead, I walk one to five miles every day. Exercise produces the same happy hormones you would get from an antidepressant. That has worked well. I was sleeping better and became more active, and I had a more positive attitude. It was time to think about a major hike.

Another Big Hike

A year earlier, my brother and I had made reservations at the bottom of the Grand Canyon at a lodge called Phantom Ranch. I had reserved three slots for the trip. At the time, I thought I would win my immigration appeal and have two sons to take on a hike. Now we had several slots open. What was I going to do? To fill the empty slots, I asked Joe if Harvey and any of the Tucker extended family would be interested in going. My thinking at the time was for adults from the large Tucker extended family to join us. Instead, Joe arranged for Harvey, age nineteen, and two cousins, ages eleven and twelve, to hike with me across the Grand Canyon. Before things were finalized, I had the two Tucker cousins hike fourteen miles with full backpacks. They proved to themselves, as well as to myself at age fifty-eight, that the four of us had the mental and physical stamina to hike across the Grand Canyon.

For two weeks, I would be fully responsible for

Harvey and his two young cousins. Other than meeting my brother at the canyon, I would be on my own with these three boys, the closest I will ever come to my dream of a dad-and-sons Grand Canyon adventure.

Yes, Harvey, his two cousins, and I did hike across the Grand Canyon. The hike was a dream come true after 25 years; thanks to Joe Tucker & his son Harvey.

North Rim entrance to Grand Canyon

North Kiabab Trail Head; ready to start hike

Harvey and his two cousins; North Kiabab Trail

Just north of Cottonwood ranger station

Phantom Ranch

GARRY WHITE

Two cousins water fight; Indian Gardens

South Rim of Grand Canyon—we made it across!

Ceremony of Loss

The day finally arrived for my ceremony of loss. For me, it was a funeral to allow me to grieve for the sons I will never have. My brother, his wife, my nephew, Joe, his wife, Ann, and my therapist were there at the banks of the Blanco River. I also grieved for Matt, the young man I had to walk away from in order to get him to help himself, and for Mark, the foster son I had to give up since he needed a better placement. At the river, I had a picture of Mount San Francisco outside of Flagstaff where I made the decision to give up Mark. And there was Luke (Jerry), the boy who was to be my son. He was the reason I had signed myself into a psychiatric hospital.

At the end of three balloons were pictures I had of each of these boys. While the others looked on, I walked down to the river and released the balloons with their pictures. All I remember is my brother acknowledging that thirty years of trying had come to an end.

After the ceremony, breakfast waited at my apartment, prepared by the Tucker boys. During breakfast, I gave my business card to each of the Tucker family sons, a symbol that they could call me if they ever needed help. In a way, it was a symbolic gesture marking them as mine. I had planned to do this with my adopted sons. They were to have my contact information with them at all times in case of an emergency.

After everyone left, I took a pill to sleep off the

stress. When I woke up in the late afternoon, I started working on this book and planning the Grand Canyon trip with Harvey and his two young cousins.

You see, I never give up.

Section 504 and Me

When I left my lawyer's office, I was very depressed. Four licensed mental health practitioners had indicated that my mental history should carry no weight and that I was qualified as a candidate for an international adoption. It all seemed unfair. As I got into my car, I thought about Section 504. During my treatment for anxiety twenty-four years ago, someone told me about Section 504 of the 1973 Rehabilitation Act.

The federal law states that a history of mental illness cannot be used to deny a qualified candidate services or opportunities. From the Internet, I learned this was true and that the Department of Homeland Security (DHS), Office for Civil Rights and Civil Liberties ensures that federal agencies within DHS, such as Immigration, comply with this law.

I decided to renew the battle without the help of

my friends and family, aside from my lawyer, since the ceremony of loss was already planned. Here is the letter I sent in January of 2008:

Department of Homeland Security
Office for Civil Rights & Civil Liberties
Review & Compliance Unit
Washington DC 20528

SUBJECT: Protection under Sec 504, Reh Act 1973

Dear Review and Compliance Officer:

I request protection under Section 504 of the Rehabilitation Act of 1973 and Title II of the Americans with Disabilities Act of 1990. I have a history of mental illness. It is unfairly being used against me. I am a qualified candidate for an international adoption.

In 1983, I had an anxiety attack that resulted in two psychiatric hospitalizations. Dr. Joug, psychiatrist, treated me successfully. For the past several years, I have been trying to adopt internationally. On December 27, 2007, the Immigration Administrative Appeals Office (AAO) denied my I-600A application appeal. Decision brief is enclosed. The reason for dismissal and application denial was from an old home study by Rimstone Adoption Agency. It stressed my psychiatric illness twenty-four years ago. Most of the negative comments were based on the "impressions" of the caseworker.

Four licensed mental health practitioners (attending psychiatrist, current family therapist, and two clinical and forensic psychologists) indicate that 1) my history of mental illness should carry no weight in any decisions involving my ability to parent, and 2) I am psychologically and emotionally fit to be an adoptive parent.

It was wrong for the AAO to use my mental history as grounds for dismissal and application denial.

Requested Action:

I) The Immigration Service disregards the May 2004 Rimstone Adoption Agency home study on the grounds:

    1. It is outdated and incomplete.

    2. It ignores the conclusions, opinions, and recommendations from two licensed mental health practitioners (attending psychiatrist and current family therapist).

    3. It lacks any psychological assessment.

II) The Immigration Service accepts the August 2006 home study by Parent Maker (enclosed) on the grounds:

    1. It is more current and complete.

    2. Accepts the conclusions, opinions, and recommendations from four licensed mental health practitioners (attending psychiatrist, current family therapist, and two clinical and forensic psychologists).

3. Supported by two psychological assessments.

4. Supported by an earlier home study (Dec 2004) by another caseworker.

III) The Immigration Service provides me an official document indicating approval for two brothers, ages eight to eleven, from Ukraine or Russia.

IV) The Immigration Service contacts Flowstone International Adoption Agency stating something similar to the following:

> In 2004, you accepted Garry White as an applicant for an adoption from Russia. When your office found out that the Immigration Service canceled his I-600A application, you also canceled his application. The Immigration Service decision was a mistake. This mistake should carry no weight in any decisions dealing with Garry White. His new I-600A application has been approved for two brothers, ages 8–11, from either Ukraine or Russia. Even though he is four years older, now age 57, we advise you to re-instate Garry White as your applicant as he was in 2004.

A week after my letter and documents arrived in the Review and Compliance Unit, there was no acknowledgment. I phoned. The clerk said I should hear something in two weeks. After three weeks, there was no acknowledgment. I phoned again. The clerk stated the office had received my letter and supporting documents and that I should hear something soon.

After another three weeks, I called again to find out the time frame for acting on my case. The clerk said she would have the investigator call me back the next day. After another week without a returned call, I phoned again. I was told to call back the next day after nine a.m. to speak to the investigator. The next day I was put on hold for ten minutes. I hung up and called back again. She said she would call me back within a day. Another week passed with no response. I tried the phone number for the main Civil and Liberties DHS office four times. It was always a quiet "please hold" voice, and I was put on hold before I could say something. After about five or ten minutes, I hung up. My e-mails also drew no replies. All I wanted to know was when the Review and Compliance Unit would start on my case.

About three weeks later, I again sent an e-mail to the Review and Compliance Unit and a certified letter to the Office for Civil Rights and Civil Liberties in the Department of Homeland Security. My communications stated that it had been three months, and there had been no official reply. I asked how long it usually took between receiving a request and acting on it. No reply.

Finally, after another month, I contacted my congressman to find out the status of my case. About two weeks later, I received a letter from the Office for Civil Rights and Civil Liberties (CR and CL). The letter stated,

After carefully reviewing your information, our Office has determined that U.S. Citizenship and Immigration Services (USCIS) must provide us with additional information regarding your allegation before a determination can be made. When we have received all the appropriate documentation from USCIS, we will carefully review it, make a determination as to how your matter should be handled, and inform you in writing of our decision.

Nine months after receiving the Office for CR and CL letter stating Immigration needed to provide information, Immigration had yet to reply to the Office of CR and CL. This is what the CR and CL investigator told me over the phone.

After a year, on February 23, the CR and CL investigator phoned me and stated that he had received documents from Immigration. His goal was to send me a response within thirty days.

After sixty days, on April 23, I sent an e-mail and letter stating that I had yet to hear their response. On April 28, the investigator left a message on my phone that a response had been sent. He did not say when. I immediately sent another e-mail and registered letter asking when it had been sent and if they could e-mail me their response.

Two weeks later, with no reply either by e-mail or letter, I contacted my congressman for help. The next day, May 14, I received via e-mail the CR and CL response. The response was dated March 23. The e-mail stated that it had been sent on March 23. I had not received it after almost two months. Here is the CR and CL response:

> "After careful review of your information and the "Decisions," issued on February 8, 2006 and April 27, 2007 by USCIS AAO, this Office has determined that USCIS addressed your allegations. Accordingly, this Office is closing your complaint as of the date of this letter."

No other explanation was given. Two days later I sent an e-mail requesting an explanation. None has been given.

After thirty-plus years of trying, I have learned I committed an unforgivable sin in 1983. How else do you explain one Rimstone caseworker's opinion carrying more weight than:

1. Attending psychiatrist, Dr. Joug
2. Attending family therapist
3. Clinical/forensic psychologist requested by Immigration, Dr. Anderson
4. Second clinical/forensic psychologist, Dr. Rogers
5. Psychological assessment requested by Immigration
6. Second psychological assessment that is consistent with the first

7. Approved international home study by a licensed master's level social worker
8. Second approved international home study by another licensed master's level social worker
9. References Immigration requested
10. Rimstone-approved domestic home study

Even if that one Rimstone caseworker was correct five years ago, today she is wrong. People do change and improve for the better when they seek help.

As my licensed therapist stated in his response to the USCIS AAO decisions, the Federal government is functioning in the "dark ages" of ignorance.

Another Child Victim

As we approach the close of this book, I want to discuss what Rimstone Adoption Agency and Immigration consider the main issues against me, what happened in 1983 during a pre-placement adoption visit, and why it happened, and whether it could happen again. Let's look back to 1983.

After my foster son, Mark, left me for a placement better suited to his needs, I proceeded with an adoption. After a pre-adoption visit with Luke (Jerry), I had an anxiety attack. With the encouragement of my parents and a close friend, I voluntarily admitted myself into a psychiatric hospital. It was the hardest thing I ever did. The issue came down to whether I should act in my own best interest (not admit myself so I could keep Luke) or act in my son's best interest (admit myself and most likely lose

Luke). I acted in Luke's best interest. As I signed the papers to admit myself, I cried.

Even if you are mentally ill, you still can act in the best interest of others. To this day, I know I made the right decision. Unfortunately, to many it was an unforgivable sin. Licensed mental health practitioners are ignored.

My first psychiatrist misdiagnosed me and prescribed the wrong medication. There was a second episode to the hospital. My second psychiatrist diagnosed me correctly and started me on stress-management therapy and got me on an as-needed anti-anxiety medication. My current therapist refined the diagnoses by adding that the incident was a panic attack, a specific form of an anxiety attack. This type of mental illness is a situational and transient illness. He said that it was caused by my failure with my foster son, Mark. Emotionally, I feared that I would fail again with my adoptive son, Luke. My therapist was almost correct. Mark was a minor contributor to my anxiety attack.

A few years ago, I heard on TV that the police rescued a kidnapped teenage boy from years of captivity with a kidnapper. This story caught my attention. As the teen and his parents appeared on a TV news conference the next day, I noticed that the teenager had a ring on his lip, a piercing on his earlobe, and messy hair. He looked like an antisocial street kid. As the news conference proceeded, I also noticed that this teenager and parents were exchanging obvious signals of affection. That is not the behavior of street kids. This did not make sense. It then dawned on me: Matt! Everything Matt had told me was there on the TV screen. I started to have the same red flags I had in 1983, obsessively thinking about Matt and this teenager. It was becoming hard to concentrate on other things, like eating. I felt as though I was having another anxiety attack. I immediately told my therapist about my conversations with Matt and how angry I was that people did not understand why this teenager had never escaped, even when the kidnapper was gone and he had access to a phone. My therapist pointed out that, for the years that I had been seeing him, this was the first time I talked about Matt.

As we explored my emotional reaction to this rescued teenager, it became clear that Matt was the major cause of my anxiety attack in the fall of 1983. My failure to help him after years of trying and my having to eventually walk out of his life in the spring of 1983 affected me deeply. Both Matt and Mark were kids from Child Protective Services, just like Luke. Hence, I became anxiety-ridden at the thought of dealing with children from Child Protective Services. There was no anxiety working with John and the other Scouts at the youth correctional facility, only positive feelings. When I looked into international adoption, there was no anxiety thinking of the kids from Eastern Europe, again only positive feelings. Why? The YCF kids and international adoption kids were different situations. I was not dealing with children from Child Protective Services.

When I left my therapist, I asked my primary care physician to prescribe medication to help me sleep. That evening, I spent the night at the Tucker family home. Seeing their boys home and safe in their beds made me feel better.

The next night, two old college friends, Jess and Leo, came for a weekend of TV football and fishing. I provided the crash pad. They provided me a Mexican chicken mole dinner. When they arrived, they saw I was sad for some reason and asked if they should leave. I told them no; I needed their company this weekend especially. So we did the things we had planned to do for that weekend. We kidded, laughed, talked about old times, and watched football. They made me chicken mole—enough for the next week. I told them about the kidnapped teenager and how that situation was bothering me.

Thanks to my medical team, my friends, and lots of chicken mole, I was back to my old self in less than a week. In light of this episode, were Rimstone Adoption Agency and Immigration correct? Or were the four licensed mental health practitioners, two other caseworkers, and references correct? *You, the reader, decide.*

Thinking about that poor captive kid, I still get angry. I was furious when a TV commentator said the reason the teenager had never escaped was that he actually liked the lifestyle. I'd like to share with that commentator what Matt told me about that lifestyle, nothing left to the imagination, and explain why it was physically impossible for the teenager to escape. I told two friends that this teenager would have been better off being murdered than to live the hellish lifestyle. Later, at another interview, the teenager told a reporter he sometimes thought death was better then what he was going through.

One friend got mad because I did not tell what was getting me so upset. He demanded I tell him. So I did. I told him what Matt told me with details and nothing left to the imagination, including methods of torture that left no body marks. That was a mistake. Two days later, this friend told me he was having problems sleeping because of what I had told him. Luckily, I did not tell him methods of torture that did leave body marks. Such stories of what these kids experience will drive anyone insane.

The main reason this teenager never escaped, even when the kidnapper was gone and he had access to a phone, was fear. There is also the sense of helplessness, the belief that he could do nothing. The fear was so great that even if he was with a policeman without the kidnapper, he still was terrified. What if the police did not believe him? The kidnapper could say his son was antisocial and rebellious. Who do you think the police would believe: a street kid or a businessman, a known and respected member of the community? The teenager believed, with good reason, that had he gone to the police or told neighbors, and the police or the neighbors did not believe him, he would be killed. In fact, it was made known that the kidnapper did try to kill the teenager at one time. Bear in mind that the neighbors might tell the respected member of the community how his son was making up stories about being kidnapped. Obviously, when his son disappears, the kidnapper would tell the neighbors his antisocial, rebellious son ran away from home.

As long as the kidnapper was free in the streets, the teenager would still be in fear of his life. I noticed that the TV stations showed a lot of clips of the kidnapper in jail clothes, chained, and surrounded by police. I hope this made the teen feel safer.

I believe there was more to why this teenager was unable to escape. As Matt put it, the "leash" prevents a child from escaping. With the facial piercing of the lip and earlobe and other markings, such as messed-up hair, people will tend not to listen to the child. It was physically impossible to escape from the facial piercing. It all goes back to fear and helplessness. As the teenager and Matt said, they were scared.

EPILOGUE: THE BEST AND TRUE DAD

My Comparison to a Two-Parent Family

Yes, older adoptive children from Eastern Europe do bring with them emotional and mental problems. My point is that I am more knowledgeable and ready than most two-parent adoptive families.

I have a master's degree in psychology and have taken graduate courses in adolescent psychology and special education. The state has certified me to teach in public schools. For five years, I was an assistant scoutmaster for a troop at a state youth correctional facility. I have researched problems that school-age children might have, including institutional autism, developmental delay, depression, anxiety, and sensory integration disorder, all problems well within my knowledge and abilities.

I am aware of local resources for help. There is a Russian/Ukrainian Orthodox church fifty miles away. The priest told me his parishioners will be available for any assistance. Also locally, there is the organization Families of Russian and Ukrainian Adoptions (FRUA).

There is family counseling in my town. Over the years, I have been working with a licensed family therapist who works with Child Protective Services children so I could learn how to deal with problems an adopted child might have. I have been seeing this therapist for the last eight years. For some, this proves that I have mental issues that prevent me from being a single dad. Here is my rebuttal.

One of my California cousins is a trainer. People visit her to exercise and learn how to eat better. Why? Is it because they are physically ill? Or is it because they wish to enhance their physical health to avoid physical illnesses and heart attacks? I see this therapist because I wish to enhance my mental health to avoid mental illnesses and anxiety attacks. This is called preventive medicine. How much better our society would be if everyone had the same attitude. Or is getting mental health services an unforgivable sin? Is signing oneself into a psychiatric hospital because it is in the best interest of a child a sign of a good or bad parent?

How many two-parent families prepare themselves through a family therapist? How many two-parent families have a family therapist ready to step in at the first sign of problems? And how many two-parent families realize that therapy requires the parents, too? Generally, when there are problems, parents see them only as the child's problems. My plans are to get into family therapy before problems occur.

Many times, adoptive parents of older foreign children think that therapy is useless since the child does not speak English. That is wrong. Therapy focuses on feelings and expressions. Children are less verbal, anyway. Therapy includes play and drawing, a common way for children to express themselves nonverbally.

From my research, I found that, although these school-age children have problems, only 15 percent of the placements fail. We hear horror stories of older-child adoptions. Yet there are many success stories. I know a single man in New Mexico who adopted a twelve-year-old boy from Russia. He told me there were no problems and that it was a great experience. I met a family in a Boy Scout troop near where I live who adopted an eleven-year-old boy and his thirteen-year-old sister from Russia. They are very happy.

I have communicated with other families via the Families of Russian and Ukrainian Adoptions (FRUA) Web site. I have also communicated with Robert Klose, the author of *Adopting Alyosha: A Single Man Finds a Son in Russia* (1999). He is a university biology professor in Maine.

In 2004, a single man near Abilene, Texas, e-mailed me his story. He adopted from Ukraine. Yes, there were problems with his son at first. He thought he had made a big mistake. But after a few months of adjustment, they became a very happy family. He wrote, "I urge you to go for it."

My Dreams Are Now a Fantasy

Is it wrong to have dreams and goals? The Rimstone caseworker wrote,

Although he will accept whatever number of children is deemed appropriate by Rimstone, he adamantly believes that three sons would suit him the best... Garry's determination to pursue the adoption of three older children at one time, despite stated concerns, leads this worker to believe that Garry has little understanding of how the adoption of three children will impact him emotionally, mentally, and physically... In his determination to pursue his dream of adopting three children, Garry appears to be denying any and all possible complications and hardships.

Was it wrong for a high school ninth grader who was reading and writing on a third-grade level, and had teachers telling his parents he was not college material, to be determined to pursue his dream of becoming a university professor who publishes research articles? Obviously, such a person appears to be denying any and all possible complications and hardships. University faculty has nominated me twice for outstanding researcher.

Was it wrong for a mentally ill person in a psychiatric hospital at one time, with no background or experience, to be determined to pursue his dream of taking a Boy Scout troop on a hike across the Grand Canyon, especially when Scout leaders said that was too much? Obviously, such a person appears to be denying any and all possible complications and hardships. A Boy Scout troop was the first of many groups I led across the Grand Canyon.

My dreams of being a dad, like carrying them out of the orphanage to the car, putting them to bed in their room, and reading a bedtime story, are now just fantasies.

Continuing My Quest

My brain is wired to be a dad. I still want to be a dad to three homeless boys, ages eight to thirteen. I'm almost in my sixties. As a very logical person, I know my hope is not logical. Although I will never be a dad to a few homeless boys, I will still fight the system. A mother said on TV that she would search for her kidnapped son until she dies. I will continue my quest until I die. I will have the satisfaction that I never gave up, just like a true loving dad.

APPENDIX A: MY LETTER TO RIMSTONE ADOPTION AGENCY

Dear Rimstone president, social worker, and international director:

I came to you for help. Instead, you destroyed my dream of being a single dad to two or three homeless boys. You ruined my life. You denied my now-deceased mother the joy of grandchildren. Seeing dads having quality time with their sons at the grocery store, malls, and especially at church tortures me.

The ethical and professional response to deal with my case would have been to 1) stop the home study as soon as it was determined my case would fail, 2) inform me of your concerns, 3) tell me to work with my therapist on those concerns, 4) tell me to get a psychological assessment, and then 5) reexamine the issue after one year.

Why did you ignore my therapist, a licensed mental health practitioner? After working with me for more than six years, he knows me. What stopped you from requesting a psychological assessment from a licensed forensic/clinical psychologist? A third professional opinion would have been a good idea.

In my religion, we try to help people, even if they have sinned. Be not harsh in judging others. Instead, help others when help is needed. There is always hope for those who sincerely try to do right, improve, and seek professional help. We all have an obligation toward such people. You have the opportunity to learn from your mistakes without fear of consequences. Remember, there is dignity and honor in learning from your mistakes.

I urge you to follow the example of European Adoption Consultants (EAC). That agency rejected me twice. Yet the caseworker tried to help me with guidance, and the director saw to it that the reasons for the rejections were clearly explained to me. EAC is not affiliated with any religious groups. But that agency was very Christian to me. You need religious guidance. I urge you to get an ordained minister or priest on your staff.

Sincerely,
Garry L. White

APPENDIX B: TIPS TO BECOME A SINGLE ADOPTIVE DAD

Unfortunately, there is still ignorance, prejudice, and stereotyping in our society toward single men. Here are my tips if you wish to be a single adoptive dad.

1. First, work with a family therapist to make sure you are ready and able to show warmth and feelings.
2. Get a psychological assessment.
3. Get involved in Scouting, take Wood Badge, and get with a good unit where the boys run the meeting and decide campouts and activities—*not* the adults.
4. Be involved with your friends' kids and extended family's kids. If two or more of them spend a few weeks with you, you will have a good idea of how your life will change. This will sound good to the caseworker.
5. Become a CASA volunteer for a year. You are a court-appointed advocate for a child in Child Protective Service (CPS). You visit and get to know all about the child and make a recommendation to the judge. You will learn a lot about abused and neglected children under the care of CPS. It will give you

an idea of where these children come from, domestically or internationally. This will look good to any caseworker.

6. Be established in your church. Maybe teach Sunday school.

7. Do your homework. Be very knowledgeable and do not show it. This will help you select a good, honest home study agency and a good, honest placement agency. And you will have a good idea of what will fit you. Learn as much as you can about the system, where the kids come from, and their general background, problems, and issues. Read the book *Attaching in Adoption* by Deborah Gray. Another good book to read is *How It Feels to be Adopted* by Jill Krementz. Showing some of this knowledge will impress the caseworker.

8. Select your references carefully. It is not what they say. It is how they say it. Everyone you ask will be polite. Did they say yes, or did they say, "Yes!"?

9. Be sure your extended family is a "Yes!" If there is a lack of enthusiasm, you have to get them on your side before approaching a home study agency. Research shows that extended family attitudes on adoption influence the success of a placement.

10. You may want to foster care for six months. It will give you a good idea of what to expect

in being a parent to a child from the system. The best acceptable excuse for ending foster care is that Child Protective Services returned the child to the parents. The next best reason is that you committed to six months only to better prepare yourself for an adoption. Any other reasons will look bad. If you have problems and ask the child to leave, no matter what the reason, that will look very bad. Therefore, be careful in being a foster parent. If you turn down too many referrals, that will look bad too.

Be sure you understand the difference between foster care and adoption. You may find yourself in an awkward position. Why not foster instead of adoption? You are still doing parent things. There is a greater need for foster parents than adoptive parents. Foster care involves making a commitment to the life of a child. Adoption involves making a lifelong commitment to a child. There is a difference between being a temporary parent for the present and a permanent parent into the future. A relationship between foster parents and child continuing, after the child leaves, is a rare occurrence.

11. Once all of the above is done, you can now search for an agency that does only home studies, no placements. Such an agency will be local, and it will be easy to meet the caseworker personally.

Working with a local agency that does only home studies will give you flexibility with placement agencies, which will most likely be out-of-town or out-of-state. It is hard to meet with them personally. If one placement agency gives you problems, you can go elsewhere. It is much harder to go to another placement agency if the first placement agency did your home study. Here are things to consider with selecting and working with a local agency for a home study:

a. Select a local home study agency you can trust. European Adoption Consultants (EAC) can refer you to a home-study-only agency you can trust.

b. Again, do your homework. Remember, just because the person you talk to is licensed and in an honorable profession does not mean that person cannot mislead you or outright lie.

c. Check with the Better Business Bureau about the agency.

d. Check online chat rooms involving adoptions. See what is said about that agency. The FRUA Web site is a good source for such information.

e. Personal contact with a caseworker is better than sending a letter with documents. Call and make a personal appointment with the caseworker or director. When you first meet the caseworker or director, present your psychological assessment, a letter from your family therapist, letters from your references and family, and a short resumé of your activities with children (i.e. Scouting, Sunday school, foster care, Big Brother program, etc.).

f. Ask for references from the agency, especially references from single men.

g. Be careful of the social worker putting words in your mouth. If it is negative, reject what was said.

h. If the caseworker seems to be very negative with questions, nothing positive is being recorded. Stop the study and go elsewhere.

i. If the caseworker lies or tells you to do something that does not feel right to you, find another agency.

j. If asked what type of child problems you cannot accept, focus on the problems you will accept. If pressured for what you will not accept, say problems that require a very high level of care such as residential treatment. If possible, have reasons. The best answer is, "If I see the child as mine, problems will not matter."

k. Focus on the needs of the child, not your needs.

l. Express warmth. A therapist can help you with that. This is very important. Remember, the decision is based on how the caseworker feels about you, not the facts.

m. Be prepared for the question, "How do you satisfy your sexual desires?"

n. Be prepared for the question, "Why do you want to adopt?" This is a very critical question. Speak from your heart. The caseworker will be listening to how you answer.

12. Avoid Russia. A U.S. Embassy staff member there will block your application. You are better off with the Ukraine. The government and U.S. Embassy there are more single-men-friendly.

13. Once you get an approved home study and a good psychological assessment, submit an application to Immigration if international. The form will ask for the placement agency. Just put "to be determined." You'll get that information to Immigration once you find a placement agency. When you get Immigration approval, you have your paperwork ready and can start looking for a placement agency.

14. Finding a placement agency is much the same as finding a home study agency. Most likely,

the placement agency will be out of town or out of state. When you approach an agency, you must be very careful. Be relaxed and easygoing. If you appear desperate or highly emotional, you'll lose. Attending an adoption fair would be best so they can meet you and see what you are really like. Otherwise try to phone the agency to arrange an appointment to discuss your interests and to give them your documents: approved home study, references, psychological assessment, letter from your therapist, and immigration approval. It is a waste of time trying to get an agency to work with you once they say no. Go elsewhere.

From my experience, unfortunately, I suspect that fewer than 10 percent of domestic or international agencies work with single men. There are a few out there. FRUA and your local home study caseworker can give you leads.

My hopes are that these tips 1) will be of some help to those who wish to adopt, and 2) will provide insight to adoption agencies and caseworkers as to the issue of single men wishing to be dads. Remember, if a male monkey can adopt a distressed juvenile monkey, a single man can adopt a distressed juvenile child too.

BIBLIOGRAPHY

Gray, D. (2002). *Attaching in Adoption: Practical Tools for Today's Parents.* Perspectives Press, Inc., Indianapolis, Indiana.

Harlow, H. & Harlow, M. (1966). Learning to Love. *American Scientist,* 54(3), 244–272

Klose, R. (1999). *Adopting Alyosha: a Single Man Finds a Son In Russia.* University Press of Mississippi, Jackson, Mississippi.

Krementz, J. (1983). *How It Feels to be Adopted.* Alfred A. Knopf, New York, New York.